THE WILD MENU

THE WILD MENU

Recipes from the Original National Wild Game Cooking Competition

By Chef Christopher Ray
with Greg Linder

WILLOW CREEK PRESS
Minocqua, Wisconsin

Acknowledgments

A great many people deserve thanks and gratitude for helping *The Wild Menu* and the Original National Wild Game Cooking Competition become realities. These people in my life know who they are, and I hope I remind them often of my appreciation.

A special thanks to:

Mr. and Mrs. James Ray, for always believing and to Mom for always standing behind me, no matter what.

Denny and Rene Johnstone, for being involved and supporting the origin of the National Wild Game Cooking Competition

David Weber, for putting faith in this project and others we've dreamt up.

The staffs at the Flat Creek Eatery and Saloon and the Country Inn and Suites, and to my chef staff for wanting to learn so much and being so eager to help.

Carl Nordberg, for his friendship and exuberance.

Greg Linder, for his patience and expertise.

Tom Miller, for being the principal chef in starting my career.

Willow Creek staff, for taking this project and running with it.

Ed and Rosa Hoppe, whose expertise with the camera and hospitality are parallel to none.

Chef Ron Bohnert, for showing me "the way" with food, and for his friendship.

All the chefs in North America who are "cooking the game." After all, this competition is for YOU!

My siblings, Debra, Jim, Theresa and Eileen, for getting and keeping me going.

Grandpa Fred, for the inspiration from you, the "great cook," on the tugboat in the Pacific Northwest.

All the chefs who have made the journey to compete in the National Wild Game Cooking Competition in Hayward, Wisconsin. You have made it what it is. Thanks for the many great memories.

My wife Karen, for without her great love and everlasting support, I would be nowhere. She deserves the greatest credit of all. Thanks for believing and always being there.

My children, James (J.C.) Ray, Cherie Armstrong, Jacob Ray and Zachary Stevens Ray, my greatest inspirations!

Photography: Cover, page 2, and page 6 by Ed Hoppe.
Photographs from the 1995 Competition by Paul Skrentny.

ISBN 1-57223-037-1

Published by WILLOW CREEK PRESS
PO Box 147, Minocqua, WI 54548
For information on other Willow Creek titles, write or call 1-800-850-WILD.

For more information on the Original National Wild Game Cooking Competition, call or write:

ATTN: Chef Christopher P. Ray
Original National Wild Game Cooking Competition
Flat Creek Eatery & Saloon, c/o The Country Inn & Suites
P.O. Box 1010
Hayward, WI 54843
(715) 462-9008 or 800-833-4100

Thanks to Davee Schuh of Valley Game and Gourmet, Salt Lake City, Utah, for providing the food shown on the cover.

Contents

Wild Game: The "New" Cuisine

Half of human invention, it seems, is nothing more than the resurrection of ideas. If an idea falls out of favor for a sufficient period of time, some enterprising individual inevitably rediscovers it. If the idea catches on, observers are likely to hail it as a "new" and progressive trend. We see this phenomenon in the fashion world—your grandmother's dress from the 1940s seems to mimic the cut and fabric of the newest creations emerging from Paris. Or is it the other way around?

The recycling of ideas happens in the culinary world as well, and so it is that wild game cuisine has been regarded as a "new" development in cooking and dining since the late 1980s. No matter that wild game was a dietary staple for generations of hunting and gathering Native Americans. Never mind that wild game served as a primary food source for European settlers in America. Sensible chefs and food devotees simply shrug off the irony and savor the palette of delicious, healthy wild game creations now available after a long absence from the mainstream American menu.

Chef Christopher Ray, the 34-year-old founder of the Original National Wild Game Cooking Competition held annually in Hayward, Wisconsin, has paid close attention to the culinary developments of recent years. With other young chefs, he has become a champion of the "new traditionalism" that wild game represents. "How many of us grew up with game on the table?" he asks. "Not many. So it is new to most of us. We sometimes think we're setting the world on fire with this trend, but in truth we're just looking back."

There is one respect, however, in which today's wild game practices differ from those of the past. Historically, diners thought of venison in the fall, because that's when the hunting season occurred. Today, however, venison and other wild game meats are available year-round—and the quality remains consistent.

In the United States, wild game was revitalized when a recent wave of European chefs came to America, bringing with them an array of dishes prepared with venison, pheasant, wild boar, squab, and other game species. Most of these recipes had never fallen off of European menus. The number of such chefs, however, was relatively small, and they encountered resistance from customers unaccustomed to such "exotic" cuisine. Serving wild game was regarded as risky, but it could be rewarding if a restaurant's clientele was receptive.

The terms "youth" and "tradition" are not often paired, but it was indeed young chefs who took the American diner's interest in wild game cuisine to another level. Many chefs began by simply converting or adapting traditional dishes to wild game—substituting quail or partridge for Cornish game hen, for example, or venison for beef. It was a non-threatening way of introducing customers to unexpected flavors and textures—the dish looked familiar, even if the meat was different. The finalists at the Original National Wild Game Cooking Competition clearly reflect the youthful trend. All five chefs were under 30 in 1994, and none of the 1995 finalists were over 35.

During the late 1980s and the early 1990s, foods and flavors were introduced at an unprecedented rate. Simultaneously, the dining public became increasingly health-conscious. Taking note of both trends, young chefs embraced wild game cuisine partly as a means of making a name for themselves in a highly competitive profession, and partly because they believed in the flavor and health benefits of wild game. The nutritional aspect is of great interest to Chef Ray, who conducts nutritional cooking classes at the Hayward Memorial Hospital and offers seminars to food purveyors and other groups. "We're not waiting until we're 55 to figure out what our cholesterol levels are," he says, happy to relay the news. "We want to be healthy and active throughout our lives." Wild game can make a contribution. As a rule, the meat from wild game species is low-fat, low-calorie, low-cholesterol, and high in protein.

—⟶⟨⟶—

It's important to emphasize that the term "wild game," as it is used in the culinary world, often refers to wild game species that are raised on farms or ranches. The advantages of eating these "domesticated" versions of wild game species are multiple, but the characteristic that first strikes many diners amounts to an absence. The "gamey" flavor traditionally associated with wild game has diminished or, in some cases, has disappeared altogether. Dishes prepared with farm- or ranch-raised game are surprisingly delicate, tender, and sweet.

Animals on commercial farms or ranches are not "wild" in the strict sense. They are bred for the sole purpose of commercial distribution, as are cows, pigs, and chickens. They are raised in humane conditions—many are allowed to roam freely over large parcels of land. They are fed a "natural foods diet" that is inarguably healthy—for both the animal and the human consumer. In effect, these animals are raised organically within a simulated natural environment. Species such as farm-raised deer also make efficient use of natural resources, as they are not prone to the overgrazing and habitat destruction that can accompany commercial beef ranching operations.

Today's commercially produced wild game can offer greater purity and a higher degree of consistency than beef, chicken, or pork. The animals are processed in a swift and sanitary manner, and at a consistent, youthful age that ensures tenderness and cleanliness. Few if any chemicals such as steroids, hormones, and antibiotics are used, because the animals are innately healthy and disease-resistant. As a result buffalo meat, for example, is considered "hypoallergenic," and can be eaten by those who experience an allergic reaction to commercial beef. Buffalo is also a viable source of protein for dieters, as it contains just 50 calories per ounce.

The key to the flavor evolution of farm- and ranch-raised game lies in controlled diet. Farm-raised deer may eat nothing but corn and grain, whereas a deer killed in the field eats whatever it can scavenge. The wild deer's random diet includes leaves, flowers, buds, acorns, and berries, but if food is scarce, the deer may resort to mucky swamp water, tree bark, rotted vegetation, and even animal excrement. As you might imagine, an animal's food intake affects the flavor of its meat.

Today, under federal law, commercially produced wild game must be raised on a farm or ranch. State and/or local inspection is generally mandated, and both the federal Food and Drug Administration and the U.S. Department of Agriculture play a role in commercial game regulation. The meat must be sold through a licensed distributor, in order to ensure rigorous compliance with health and sanitation regulations, which in turn protects the consumer from improper handling and bacterial contamination. In fact, the argument can be made that today's commercially raised wild game is safer and more rigorously inspected than domesticated meats. At the least, commercial farms and ranches are now known for providing healthy, clean, extremely uniform products. "We can count on it being good," Chef Ray says. "We don't have to ask 'Is the beef select? Is it choice? Was it an Angus steer?' We know what we're getting."

Chef Ray became something of a wild game evangelist while serving as the fine dining chef at LeCarrousel, a revolving restaurant atop the Radisson-St. Paul Hotel that offers customers a bird's-eye view of the Twin Cities skyline and the Mississippi River. His first game specialties involved relatively exotic species such as rattlesnake and alligator, but he quickly expanded his repertoire to include such dishes as moose tachinella and venison Wellington. "I knew nothing about wild game in 1987," he admits. "At first, I wrecked a bunch of meat. When you take something you've never cooked before, something that doesn't have any of the characteristics you've dealt with before, you start experimenting. Sometimes it doesn't come out the way you hoped it would. But people (at LeCarrousel) ordered it and thought it was fantastic. It was new to our customers, so it really worked!"

After gaining more experience, Chef Ray began preparing such delights as buffalo ravioli, maple-glazed, seared venison chops, quail stuffed with rabbit sausage forcemeat, antelope chops, and slow-roasted wild boar rubbed with barbecue sauce.

When he headed north to manage the Landing Restaurant at Lake Vermillion, Minnesota, Chef Ray began offering duck, quail, and rabbit entrees, combined with the wild rice, wild blueberries, and wild strawberries that are abundant in the area. He went so far as to pay his cooks for venturing into the fields to pick berries. The response from his patrons was overwhelmingly positive.

―――――――――

"Wild game was our natural, beginning food," Chef Ray notes. "If you think about frontiersmen, pioneers, pilgrims, or even cavemen, you realize they often relied on wild game for food."

Native Americans were the first to "harvest" the buffalo of the Great Plains, using virtually the entire animal—the meat, the bones, and the blessedly thick, warm hide. The first dried meat was undoubtedly buffalo, cured and dried by Native Americans as "road food" and taken with them in the fatty, energy-producing form known as jerky, or pemmican. For flavor's sake, tribal preparers might add wild grapes and cherries, corn, beans, or herbs to this portable wild game food. Pemmican did not spoil, and it could be stored for as long as five years. Early Native Americans also made watertight baskets and dropped hot coals into the water in order to boil their food. Unfortunately, many traditional tribal practices and recipes have vanished, leaving us to wonder what else the Native Americans understood about food preparation that we are not aware of.

American lifestyles changed dramatically with the dawning of the Industrial Revolution in the mid-19th century. Cities became manufacturing magnets that attracted workers in unprecedented numbers. Within a few decades, the U.S. had become a largely urbanized nation. During the same period, many wild game species had become extinct or extremely rare, due to unregulated hunting and trapping practices. As is well-known, the American bison, or buffalo, was massacred and rendered nearly extinct across the Western plains. It is not so well-known, however, that commercial meat producers played a key role in the bison's comeback (there are now over 100,000 American bison in North America). The same can be said of some decimated game bird species.

In response to the diminished variety of available species, urban consumers turned to domesticated livestock and poultry for the bulk of their meat intake around the turn of the 20th century—settling for variants of beef, chicken, and pork. For most Americans, limiting variety was far more practical than traveling 40 miles into the countryside and attempting to blunderbuss a meal.

From the mid-20th century forward, consumers became convinced that their busy lives necessitated the utmost in convenience. They began relying on foodstuffs that were pre-packaged, pre-measured, pre-processed, and pre-cooked—substances that did everything short of hopping into the grocery cart. The result at times was a post-food product that offered minimal nutrition and compromised flavor.

Today, however, it's difficult for chefs, gourmands, or accomplished home cooks to avoid encountering the world of wild game. Industry and trade magazines regularly tout the health and consistency of these meats, offer suggestions for introducing them in restaurants, and publish tantalizing recipes.

On the consumer side, many supermarkets (particularly upscale stores in large metropolitan areas), meat markets, and butcher shops carry wild game—or can order it in response to requests. "Any butcher worth his salt will be able to order it for you," according to Chef Ray. Mail-order suppliers can also be an excellent source of wild game, although shipping costs add to the expense. Game can be obtained either frozen or fresh, and the shipping time between order placement and arrival amounts to two days or less in most cases. A list of wild game purveyors is included in a later section of *The Wild Menu*.

Taste and nutrition aside, perhaps the greatest pleasure associated with preparing and eating wild game is a romantic, intangible one. As John Ash and Sid Goldstein observed in *American Game Cooking*, the smell and flavors of wild game are "a reassurance of the blessings of another time and place."

Virtually any non-domesticated animal can be considered wild game, and Chef Ray has been approached by purveyors of such exotics as lion, seal, zebra, and giraffe. Although these are served in the U.S. on occasion, he has respectfully declined the offers.

It should be noted that a number of factors affect the flavor, texture, and tenderness of the meat that ultimately ends up on your plate. First off, the species of the animal is significant. A greenhead mallard, for example, will not taste like a teal, even though both are species of duck. The age and size of the animal at time of harvest is an important factor, as is the animal's "lifestyle"—its diet and environment. How the animal was processed may be the most significant variable— a field-dressed deer processed a day or two after the kill will not provide the same quality of venison offered by a farm-raised deer processed immediately after harvest in a controlled environment. Finally and obviously, preparation techniques also affect the culinary outcome.

The following feathered and furred species are those featured in the recipes that were submitted to the Original National Wild Game Cooking Competition and chosen for inclusion in *The Wild Menu*. Some are more commonly consumed than others, but all have been served at renowned American restaurants. The descriptions of flavor and texture assume that the animal is selected, processed, and prepared under optimal circumstances.

DEER (Venison). The term "venison" traditionally referred to meat gathered from virtually any hunted game. Today, however, most apply it to the meat of various species of deer.

There are 40 recognized species and many sub-species of deer, but the most common venison served in the U.S. is red venison (called cervenna) derived from farm-raised Scottish red deer. Paradoxically, most of this meat comes from deer raised in New Zealand. Thanks to perfected technology and government support of the deer farming industry, that country exports in excess of ten million pounds of venison worldwide per year, and venison has become the fastest-growing item on the wild game menu. About 75 percent of all venison eaten in the United States comes from New Zealand, although this has begun to change due to the growth of the deer farming industry in the U.S. Species from which commercial venison is produced also include white-tailed deer, sika deer, axis deer, and fallow deer. The first deer farms appeared in China some 3,000 years ago.

Those familiar with the meat of hunted deer often describe its flavor as "gamey" or "musky." By contrast, farm-raised varieties offer a civilized, herbal flavor similar to low-fat, unmarbled beef, together with a firm but velvety texture. Part of the difference is explained by the wild deer's lifestyle and its reaction to being hunted. As previously noted, wild deer have an irregular diet determined by the food available within their habitat. Wild animals also use their muscles to a much greater extent than their farm-raised counterparts, which translates into tougher meat. And finally, a deer that meets death on the wrong end of a hunter's rifle often releases large quantities of adrenaline in its final moments—part of the instinctive "fight or flight" reaction. The adrenaline itself can contribute to a gamey or acidic flavor that becomes evident when the meat is eaten.

On average, venison has less than two percent fat content. It contains less than one-third the calories of an equivalent amount of beef, and it is quite low in cholesterol. "The king of game meats" is now widely available at prices that make it a bargain in light of its flavor and nutritional profile.

MOOSE. The Cervidae (deer) family includes deer, elk, caribou, reindeer, and moose. The moose is essentially the world's largest deer, standing up to 7-1/2 feet tall at the shoulders and weighing over 1,800 pounds when full-grown. The animal's meat is dark and coarsely grained, known for its intense, concentrated flavor. Unlike beef cattle, which are often "speed-fattened" and harvested by the time they are 16 months old, moose are usually eaten at a much older age—perhaps three or four years old. The result is a more "mature" dining experience as well, meaning that the meat has achieved maximum flavor and succulence. Beef eaters should be so lucky!

ELK. The elk is the second-largest member of the deer family. Among the many red meats that can be mistaken for beef, elk meat nonetheless has distinguishing characteristics. Elk is very dark and coarsely grained, and it lacks the marbling associated with beef. Enthusiasts describe it as the sweetest of the deer meats.

CARIBOU. Caribou live in the northern regions of North America, and most of the caribou available commercially are culled from herds and processed in Canada. The relatively small animal is closely related to the reindeer. Its meat is finely grained, and resembles veal or antelope in flavor and texture.

ANTELOPE. Although antelopes look like deer, they are actually members of an animal family that includes goats and oxen. Most species are native to Africa or Asia. Mild-tasting and finely grained, antelope meat is similar to venison in terms of preparation, although the animal itself is considerably smaller than a typical deer. You might think of antelope as a tastier version of veal. Blackbuck antelope, a native of India and Nepal now raised elsewhere, is the most commonly served variety. Among its virtues: Antelope has just one-third the calories of beef.

BUFFALO (Bison). The American bison is a member of the Bovidae family, and is believed to have descended from wild cattle. Another sweet and succulent meat, buffalo has far less marbling and fat than beef, making it a healthier alternative. Bison "tastes like beef wants to taste," according to fans, but only if it is prepared correctly. Because the meat is so lean, it should be seared quickly on high heat or, if an outdoor grill

is used, grilled at 275 degrees rather than 325 or 350 degrees.

Widely hailed as "the new beef" when it reappeared on the scene, buffalo meat has been less successful than expected, in part because consumers have not known how to prepare it properly. If cooked in the same manner as beef, the result is a dry, leathery product that inevitably disappoints the diner. The lesson—for consumers and commercial producers alike—is that only through education can this healthy, delicious product come to be fully appreciated. There's an even simpler lesson that applies to a number of species, not just buffalo: Don't overcook wild game.

Sometimes called "the original health food," buffalo meat is now part of some restricted medical diets. It contains just 40 milligrams of cholesterol per 100-gram cooked serving, about half the amount found in lean beef. Marinating the meat, rubbing it, and other special preparation techniques are no longer necessary, due to the quality and purity of farm-raised bison.

MUSK OX. A shaggy cousin of the buffalo, the musk ox inhabits the Arctic coastal regions of Canada and Greenland. Northern Canada provides most of the animals currently available, but the processing methods are relatively primitive, resulting in a meat that offers a rich, intense flavor.

BEAR. Bears are the largest carnivores that roam the earth, and the Alaskan brown bear is the largest of the seven bear species. Occasionally available in markets, bear meat is coarse, dark, marbled, and about as fatty as pork. It can be prepared in a similar manner, but the cooked meat more closely resembles beef in its texture and flavor. Bear meat lends itself well to roasting, but it is less suited to sautéing or grilling. Its intense flavor is best when married to just the right sauce. A bear roast or bear chili can be particularly delicious.

WILD BOAR. A "porkier pork," wild boar is known for its sweet, nutty, and intense flavor. The nuts and greens in its diet undoubtedly account for the nuttiness of the meat when cooked. Boar meat is a deeper red than pork, and is somewhat less fatty. The meat of the young boar is truly tender, but older animals present a tougher meat characterized by a much gamier taste. The wild pigs that inhabit the southwestern United States, called javelinas or peccaries, are only distantly related to the farm-raised boars in other parts of the country. The meat is best when it comes from a boar whose dressed carcass weight is between 40 and 75 pounds.

RABBIT and **HARE**. In European butcher shops, rabbit outsells all other meats. As has been widely noted, the versatile, finely textured rabbit meat parallels chicken in flavor and texture. Rabbit meat is easy to work with and entirely digestible. Wild hare (most commonly meaning snowshoe hare or jack rabbit) should be cooked differently than rabbit, and the taste is a bit more on the wild side—earthier, gamier, chewier. Hares are generally larger than rabbits, reaching a size of up to 12 pounds. A claim to fame for both meats is that they contain almost no fat. They are widely available from suppliers, reasonably priced (due to the animals' prolific breeding habits), protein-rich, and calorie-stingy.

RATTLESNAKE. A great deal of rattlesnake meat is eaten in the western United States—where, conveniently, many rattlesnakes live. In parts of the Far East, market shoppers routinely scrutinize baskets of live snakes, choose one that meets their requirements, and watch as the reptile is skinned and packaged. The meat is light and chewy, with a delicate flavor that resembles chicken. Rattlesnake chili is a favorite dish at a number of restaurants in the southwestern U.S. The meat may be too expensive for moderate budgets, due to extravagant demand and a paucity of suppliers.

ALLIGATOR. Hunting of alligators for commercial purposes is now permitted (although tightly regulated) in parts of the United States. These reptiles resemble overgrown lizards, and they are often confused with their relatives, the crocodiles. Although alligator meat is light, it is firm of texture and carries a strong flavor. Most wild game chefs recommend serving it with a marinade or sauce; featuring the meat in fritters, jambalayas, or stews; or using it in soup or chili. Alligator sausage, especially if prepared with Cajun spices, is a tasty exception to the rule.

DUCK. The most commonly served species of duck include greenhead mallards, canvasbacks, teal, pintails, ringnecks, gadwalls (primarily in England), and black ducks. Again, the flavor of a farm-raised duck differs from that of the wild duck primarily due to control of the bird's diet. Farm-raised ducks are raised on corn and grain, and are harvested at a uniformly early age to ensure tenderness and consistency.

Commercial duck farms start with clean eggs, which are placed in an incubator and rocked to simulate a parent's attention. Young ducks are released into a small pen and fed a nutritious poultry feed known as "corn crumble," then released to a larger pen and offered an expanded diet at a somewhat older age. When the ducks are properly raised, the result is a delicious, succulent meat with an ample breast and an adequate layer of fat. The flavor of farm-raised ducks is often described as buttery or nutty.

Cooking a duck for a long period of time at a high temperature is likely to toughen and dry out the meat, so overcooking should be avoided. Incidentally, Oriental-style duck was a favorite dish of world conqueror Genghis Khan, although it apparently did little to improve his temperament.

GOOSE. Although geese are large birds, most wild species, such as the widespread Canada goose, are quite lean. As a result, they offer a relatively small amount of meat. Goose meat is sweet, dark, juicy, and tender. The typical Christmas goose, as depicted in Charles Dickens *A Christmas Carol,* is a fatty, domesticated species called the Long Island goose. The Toulouse goose is the predominant farm-raised species, and these birds are harvested between six and eight months of age—at the peak of their flavor. Like duck, goose often tastes buttery and rich, but the goose meat tends to have a milder flavor.

WILD TURKEY. If it weren't for the wild turkey, early European colonists who ventured to America would probably have starved to death. The late chef and philosopher James Beard insisted that there is no finer eating experience than smoked wild turkey.

Wild varieties are essentially the turkey as it existed before it was bred to have a huge breast. There is no comparison between the intense flavor of a typically lean wild turkey and the relatively uninspired taste of the standard Thanksgiving tom. The difference lies primarily in its intensity—a "taste of the woods" prevails in the leaner wild bird. Wild turkeys are abundant throughout much of the United States, and they have been successfully reintroduced in the upper Midwest. Farm-raised wild turkeys can be difficult to find, but the meat is affordably priced when available.

PHEASANT. The most treasured bird among game bird species, wild pheasants must be properly prepared and of the right age if gaminess is to be avoided. The delicate flavor of farm-raised birds is subtle and pleasant, with a discernible trace of apple in many cases. Farm-raised pheasants are widely available from suppliers, and can be found in many grocery outlets and meat markets. Cook pheasant slowly at low heat; frequent basting can be beneficial.

PARTRIDGE and **GROUSE.** These two birds are grouped together because they are closely related and similar in flavor. Obtaining a true specimen of either bird, however, can be problematic. In some regions of the U.S., the partridge is known as the quail or bobwhite. New Englanders refer to the ruffed grouse as a partridge.

The meat of the grouse is generally a bit darker than that of the partridge. Both birds are likely to have a piney, savory taste tinged with gaminess—a combination that holds strong appeal for those who enjoy a hint of the natural environment in their wild game. The chukar partridge is a common domesticated variety, and an average bird weighs 10 to 14 ounces.

QUAIL. These light-fleshed birds offer meat with a delicate texture and a sweet, nutty flavor. Quail is often stuffed with a "forcemeat" due to its small size—the average bird weighs just five to six ounces. Serving quail with forcemeat offers an intriguing combination of meat flavors and textures, but the bird is also a delicacy if served on its own. The American bobwhite and the pharaoh quail are among the most popular species.

SQUAB (Pigeon or **Rock Dove).** A true delicacy, squab is succulent, but it retains the earthy flavor undertones that please many diners. The birds we call "squab" today are in fact creations of the game breeding industry. They are young, featherless pigeons (technically rock doves) that are raised in pens. Squab is rich, dark meat of delicate texture, roughly comparable in flavor to beef or liver. The average bird weighs about 14 ounces.

OSTRICH. The ostrich is the world's largest living bird, and ostrich is touted by the food media as an up and coming entry on wild game menus. However, the meat is currently limited by its commercial scarcity and its price. A good cut of the bird's red meat, properly prepared on a grill, will yield an entree that is virtually indistinguishable from a steak or beef tenderloin. Ostrich boasts a superior nutritional profile, and the meat is lower in fat than a chicken breast.

GUINEAFOWL. A close relative of the pheasant, the guineafowl is the second most popular poultry item in France. The bird offers meat that is clean and easy to prepare. Guineafowl is darker than chicken and juicier than pheasant. The bird's tough skin holds the juices in when the meat is cooked. A guineafowl is about the same size as chicken (and the bird's eggs are eaten), but it requires less cooking time.

Wine and Beer: The Second Sauce

Wild game dishes often come replete with their own sauces, but a thoughtfully chosen pour of wine or beer can heighten appreciation of delicate flavors, "colorize" the table setting, refresh the palate, or simply wash the food down in a pleasant cascade of flavor and texture. As a result, chefs, food and beverage directors, and other authorities sometimes refer to wine and beer as "the second sauce."

The Greek philosopher Lucullus is quoted as saying, "Good drinks drive out bad thoughts." Perhaps a corollary is also true: Bad wine (or beer) can create bad thoughts. Many ill-advised diners can verify this experience. So the choice of an appropriate wine or beer assumes importance as part of the overall dining experience.

However, it would seem contradictory to encourage adventures in wild game dining on the one hand, yet insist on adherence to prescribed wines and beers on the other. If, as we suspect, the primary delight of partaking in wild game cuisine lies in discovering new and tantalizing flavors—whether from an exotic truffle or rosemary oil, a compote made of sun-dried cherries, or the meat itself—then surely the pleasures of the second sauce are best enjoyed through a similar process of experimentation.

Wine authorities (some of whom, it should be pointed out, are under contract to wineries or beverage manufacturers) at one time served as the sole arbiters of taste when it came to choosing liquid accompaniments for the fine dining experience. Their more general guidelines, which have remained fixed in the public's mind for decades, include such rules of thumb as: "Choose a red wine with dark meat or a heavy pasta; select a white wine with lighter meats or seafood." This is only minimally helpful, as any visitor to a well-stocked liquor outlet soon discovers, but the experts have been happy to provide more specific advice when called upon to do so.

As a chef committed to uninhibited exploration of game cuisine, Chef Christopher Ray approaches beverages with much the same freewheeling philosophy. Although he has fashioned his own opinions on the basis of study and personal experience, when it comes right down to choosing a selection to accompany a specific dish, he describes his decision as "instinctive." He concedes that the combination of food with wine or beer in effect creates a chemical reaction inside the diner's mouth; this reaction can distort, enhance, or neutralize the flavor and texture of the dish. However, rigid adherence to one choice or another fosters a different sort of catastrophe—it can seriously diminish the joie de vivre of the dining experience, the pleasure of personal discretion.

"If you're a wine drinker," Chef Ray says, "you know what you like, and you're going to drink what you like." Even wine educators acknowledge the key role played by personal preference. Few authorities these days will turn their noses up at a diner's expressed preference for the "wrong" white or red wine with a given entree.

However, for those who prefer to mitigate absolute freedom with commonsense guidelines, we can offer a few fundamental considerations. Begin by considering the meat, the sauce, and the ingredients of your meal. What sorts of flavors will you experience? If the meat is light and the flavor delicate, a dry and subtle white wine may do nicely. If the meat is rich and red and the accompanying sauces or stuffings are bold, a forceful red wine may be your solution. "Earthy" meals—a pheasant served with wild rice or legumes, for example—can be nicely complemented by a dark ale, a stout, or a similarly rich specialty beer. Acidic or highly spiced entrees can benefit from the palate-neutralizing effect of a lighter-colored beer.

Although it may sound simplistic, a dish in which fruit is a prominent ingredient—one that includes a fruit-based compote or sauce, for example—may be complemented by a fruity wine. Barbecuing your bison? If you're feeling adventurous, consider a smoke-flavored beer. Grilling a salmon steak? Some would choose a deep red wine; others, a dark, malty beer. In general, you might think in terms of flavor intensity—match an intensely flavored meat with a full-bodied wine or beer, and a delicate entree with a subtle second sauce.

The wine and beer environment has become immeasurably more diverse in recent decades. California wines initially cracked the dominance of French and Italian vineyards, but wines from Washington State (particularly white wines) have since gained widespread acceptance, and wines from Oregon are making inroads. And because regional wineries have emerged as contenders in many parts of the country, American wine is no longer just an East and West Coast phenomenon.

However, the biggest explosion in the beverage industry involves beer. Domestic American beer, long considered a pale imitation (literally) of European and world brews, has at last come of age. "There are now connoisseurs of beer," Chef Ray observes. "People no longer say, 'Give me a can of anything.' They're starting to ask, 'Do you carry this brand?' They know where the brewery is, what the beer is made of, and what color it should be. Some Americans are even saying, 'I'll take mine at room temperature.' They know that, because of a beer's chemical make-up, it's best when served at room temperature."

Hand-crafted specialty or gourmet beers have emerged at an astonishing rate. There are beers made with wheat, rice, honey, and other previously unvisited ingredients. There are Oktoberfest beers, beers made especially for winter or summer, dark ales and light ales, and beers with provocative (if baffling) names like "Wicked Ale" or "Rhino Chasers." And there are traditional imports like Guinness Stout, Bass Ale, and others, long considered more elegant than the domestic breeds.

Due to the varying complexities, flavors, depths, colors, and degrees of richness now available, Chef Ray has been recommending beers more frequently in the past two or three years. "The differences between beers intrigue me," he says. "Beers are almost more 'natural' than wine. I often match food from the earth, like wild rice and venison, with a nice, earthy beer."

In formal settings like banquets, Chef Ray may serve four to six ounces of beer with a meal course. "Beer doesn't have to be abundant," he says. "You're drinking it for flavor. I don't feel obliged to put a full bottle of beer in front of everybody and say 'Fill up.' Instead, taste the beer. Enjoy the beer with the food. When the food's gone, the beer's gone. You don't have a half-bottle left to struggle with before you move on to the wine."

Moderate amounts of beer and wine can be combined in the same meal. "It's not uncommon anymore to serve an appetizer with beer, then move into a main course with wine. You can use both, if you're doing it right and matching it with the food," Chef Ray notes.

Essentially, then, we encourage experimentation within the realm of personal preference. "I know people who are profound red wine drinkers," Chef Ray says. "Why would they order a bottle of white wine because they're having a piece of grilled salmon? They won't. They'll match a good red with the salmon."

If you remain uncertain, a number of people can assist you in your explorations. Wine and beverage consultants sometimes offer tastings or seminars at liquor stores or restaurants. Knowledgeable personnel at wine and beer outlets can provide a great deal of information about that bottle of pinot noir or the six-pack of dark ale you're considering. Many fine restaurants school their chefs, waitstaff, and bartenders in the characteristics of wine and beer, to help customers avoid a disastrous selection (although many don't take the trouble). There are countless books on the subject of selecting wines, and a few that cover beers. As is generally the case, however, experience is the best source of knowledge. Try new approaches to the second sauce. Learn from your taste adventures. Relish your successes, and avoid repeating your failures.

<hr>

We'd stop short of calling it "the *third* sauce," but as a grand finale, Chef Ray is a staunch advocate of specialty coffee—meaning there's another decision to be made. "Let's suppose you just went through an extraordinary tasting session of food, wine, and/or beer. Now you're sitting there, reminiscing about the pleasures of the meal. You may be starting to droop a little because of all the food. The superb, rich taste of coffee brings your senses back to life. It makes you more aware of what you just experienced. A shot of coffee stimulates the memory."

Ultimately, fine dining is just that—a collection of culinary memories. As you embark upon your own exhilarating adventures, whether at home or in restaurants, don't forget to savor every taste, every nuance of texture, and every moment of the wild game dining experience.

Anthony Robles, Sous Chef at the Star Canyon Restaurant in Dallas, 1995 Grand Prize recipient with his winning plate, "Bison Strip with Ancho Chile Rub"

Guy Reinbolt going over the final, intricate presentation of his Millefeuille of Elk Saddle.

The 1995 judges sample Anthony Robles' Grand Prize dish.

Chef Kerry Leigh Heffernan, in the final preparation stages of her Wild Boar Bacon-wrapped Quail.

The Original National Wild Game Cooking Competition: A Brief History

The home of the Original National Wild Game Cooking Competition is Hayward, a northwestern Wisconsin city surrounded by more than 200 lakes. Foremost among them is the legendary Chippewa Flowage, the third-largest lake in a water-rich state. The flowage was created in 1923, when a utility company dammed the Chippewa River, backing up 11 natural lakes, nine natural rivers, and many streams and ponds, consolidating them into an artificial but beautiful 17,000-acre fishing paradise.

Called "The Chip" or "The Big Chip" by locals and in-the-know visitors, the flowage is advertised as a "musky factory" in promotional materials. In 1949, its productive waters coughed up the officially recognized world-record musky, weighing in at 69 pounds, 11 ounces, and caught by a proud angler with the born-to-fish name of Louie Spray.

The Hayward area also offers an ample supply of walleye, crappie, bass, perch, northern pike, and bluegill, but the mighty musky is the king of northwoods gamefish. It is for this feistiest of fish that Hayward, founded as a sawmill village in 1881, is legendary. Today, photographs of men (and an occasional woman or child) cradling toothy, outsized muskies line the walls of every resort, serving as a collective community logo.

If "musky" is liberally defined, the world's largest specimen rests at the National Fresh Water Fishing Hall of Fame, an institution spawned by local businessman Bob Kutz in 1960. The Hall of Fame, which features a library and a museum, attracts over 100,000 visitors each year. In the modern-day equivalent of Jonah entering the belly of the whale, the visitors climb into a hollow musky—actually a 4-1/2-story replica suspended in mid-air that required an architect, an artist, a sculptor, bridge engineers, structural steel fabricators, and half a million dollars to design and build. The interior of the musky's mouth serves as an observation platform, but the feeling is one of being . . . well, *swallowed*. This Paul Bunyan among fish is 143-1/2 feet long, dwarfing its real-life counterparts.

Hayward hosts a rollicking Musky Festival for four days in June. Come October, a world-class fishing tournament known as the Musky Challenge plays itself out, sponsored by Muskies, Inc.

To be sure, it's a lot of fuss about a fish, but the musky mystique draws vacationers by the tens of thousands. Hayward calls itself "Home of Record Muskies," and the community spares no effort in conveying the impression that all musky roads lead to Hayward.

———◦———

Once there, other dimensions of Hayward emerge, affording visitors what might be described as the total northwoods experience. The International World Championship Lumberjack Competition, a daunting test of traditional tree-climbing and axe-handling abilities, is staged in late July. Horseback riding, hiking, biking, and swimming opportunities abound. Dozens of specialty shops offer all manner of cabin furnishings, antiques, and northwoods arts and crafts. A game farm not far from town caters to sportsmen by offering guided hunts, sporting clays, and game processing.

In May, Hayward hosts the first (and perhaps the only) fishing event for disabled people, known as Fishing Has No Boundaries. Down the road apiece, in mid-July, the Lac Court Oreilles Chippewa conduct the Honor the Earth Pow-Wow, the largest traditional Indian pow-wow in North America. A mid-September event called the Chequamegon Fat Tire Festival celebrates the passion of many area residents for the pastime known as mountain biking, and is the largest off-road bike race in North America.

In late November, an undisciplined army clad in phosphorescent orange invades the town, then spreads into the woods and fields for the ten-day war game known as "the deer season," which begins on the Saturday prior to Thanksgiving. The fearsome hunters are bane to some non-hunting locals, who hide in their homes for fear of being accidentally shot; however, they are boon to the local resort and restaurant community.

Hayward's Winterfest, held in early February, includes the World Championship Snowmobile Drag Races. In 1988, the Guinness land speed record as it pertains to snowmobiles (170.078 mph) was set by one of the competitors. Later in February, North America's largest cross-country ski race comes to Hayward, attracting a bevy of aerodynamically sound skiers plus friends, families, and spectators to the American Birkebeiner. "The Birke" is a 55-mile run that finishes up on Main Street in Hayward. It is one of just 13 races that are used in determining the world's cross-country skiing champion each year.

Hayward, then, is a town for all seasons with its heart in the great outdoors. It hosts world records and world-class events that can legitimately be described as "biggest, first, longest, fastest, oldest." All of this happens, mind you, in a northern Wisconsin city with an official population of just 1,913.

And on April 23 and 24, 1993, yet another "first" was initiated in this thriving northwoods community.

————⟶≍⟵————

Chef Christopher Ray is not a northern Wisconsin native. However, he grew up in Seattle, a metropolis at the western edge of an unofficial swath of territory that stretches from northern Maine to Washington State and north into Canada—much of it popularly known as "the northwoods." The expanse of territory is united by a number of common characteristics—forests, cold winters, similar native herbs, berries, and wildlife.

In retrospect, it seems that Chef Ray was destined for the commercial kitchen. He began his restaurant career at the age of 18, gaining a thorough knowledge of seafood while working on the Seattle waterfront. His profession then took him to Spokane; to the Cocolezzone (Italian) Restaurant and the Legends Cafe in Minneapolis; to the elegant dining room known as LeCarrousel at the top of the Radisson-St. Paul Hotel (where, he says, "my culinary career began to have meaning and blossom"); to the Landing Restaurant at northern Minnesota's Lake Vermillion; and, most recently, to the Hayward area. He has won a number of awards at cooking competitions, and he is a certified member of the American Culinary Federation.

Chef Ray's tenure in Hayward began in 1991, when he became executive chef of the Dun Rovin Lodge, a rustic but first-class lakeside resort. The lodge itself houses one of the few local restaurants dedicated to fine dining. At Dun Rovin, Chef Ray quickly became known for his extraordinary wild game creations. It was not uncommon for a customer to show up at the restaurant's back door, asking what "wild special" would be featured that night.

During the summer, business at Dun Rovin is brisk and

Chef Christopher Ray, founder of the Original National Wild Game Cooking Competition

unrelenting, but the pace slows in fall and winter. In the late summer of 1992, Chef Ray proposed a wild game cooking competition to lodge owner Denny Johnstone, primarily as a means of keeping himself busy and enthused through the slow months. The cooking competition fit the northwoods ambience of the lodge and the community perfectly. Once decided upon, it underwent a dizzying evolution. First defined as a local competition, the contest soon became a statewide event, then a regional extravaganza. But why build fences around a good idea? The next evolution was only natural: The cook-off was christened the 1993 Original National Wild Game Cooking Competition.

In fall of that year, Chef Ray began soliciting financial and product support from sponsors, to ensure that the cooking competition paid for itself. He developed a list of chefs, then sent out 3,000 notices inviting them to enter recipes in the cooking competition—grand prize, $1,000. Because he didn't have a computer or a typewriter, he typed each mailing label on the Hayward Public Library's noisy, older-model IBM typewriter.

The chef began lining up judges who could astutely evaluate the chefs' presentations at the cook-off in Hayward. He intended to publicize the event by developing press releases for the media, but he didn't fancy himself an accomplished writer.

At the suggestion of a friend, Chef Ray contacted Carl Nordberg, a Minneapolis-based chef and food writer with an extensive marketing background. Nordberg's track record in sales, management, and promotion was impressive. He had in the past cultivated "image awareness" for large companies like Anheuser-Busch. A devotee of professional auto racing, he had managed Paul Newman's professional racing team for two years. He had served as the management director of a five-restaurant chain. Then, in the early 1990s, he abruptly enrolled in a vocational-technical school program to become what he had wanted to be all along—a working chef.

Chef Ray met with Nordberg in Minneapolis, outlining his plans for the cooking competition. Because of Nordberg's enthusiastic nature and his longstanding interest in cuisine,

he pledged to help the cooking competition in any way that he could—particularly by writing press releases and contacting the media. Nordberg's commitment was so immediate and wholehearted that Chef Ray at first questioned his motives. He called Nordberg from Hayward the day after their first meeting. "What do you want out of this?" he asked his would-be associate. "What kind of personal gain are you looking for?"

"Nothing," replied Nordberg. "I don't want anything. I just think it's great for the industry."

Today, three years later, Chef Ray can confidently say, "Carl Nordberg still wants nothing. He's never asked me for a thing in my life, and I'm honored to have him as a friend." A two-member team was thus established: the up and coming chef with an inspiration, and the fired-up enthusiast who could help him make it happen.

———

Barraging the media with press releases and sending personal invitations to chefs ultimately paid off; when the March, 1993, entry deadline arrived, Chef Ray and Nordberg found themselves sorting through over 150 recipes submitted by 117 chefs from around the country. Any fulltime employed chef was eligible to compete, and the chefs who sent recipes ranged from short-order cooks at franchised pancake houses to master chefs at four-star dining establishments or private mountaintop lodges. Not all of the recipes entered in that first competition were notable for their sophistication. A fair number amounted to variations on the traditional "hunter's platter," or were commonplace dishes converted to wild game; one recipe detailed the entrant's method of combining scrambled eggs and rabbit.

However, the five finalists chosen in 1993 reflected a high degree of culinary accomplishment. Ironically, one of them was Executive Chef Ron Bohnert, Chef Ray's former supervisor at the Radisson-St. Paul Hotel. The others were Mark Haugen, executive chef at Tejas, a Minneapolis restaurant; William Aschenbrenner, then the executive chef at the Broken Sound Club in Boca Raton, Florida; Jerry Peters, executive chef of the Enchantment Resort in Sedona, Arizona; and Bill Morris, sous chef at the renowned Salish Lodge in Snoqualmie, Washington. At stake were three cash prizes: the $1,000 grand prize; $500 for the runner-up; and $250 for the third-place winner. The finalists would fly into Hayward, stay for the weekend, and prepare their winning recipes for the panel of judges.

The cook-off began at noon on Saturday, April 24. The chefs prepared their dishes in Dun Rovin's small kitchen, and their artistry was documented for television broadcast by Ventures North Public Television out of Duluth, Minnesota.

At the awards banquet that evening, Chef Ray and his staff served an eight-course wild game extravaganza for the chefs and members of the public who sought a memorable dining experience, after which the winners were announced. The grand prize winner of the first annual competition was Chef Bill Morris, who dazzled the judges with his entree—a mouthwatering antelope ragout with goose prosciutto, duck sausage, lentil timbale, and potato galette. Runner-up Ron Bohnert prepared pan-seared, peppered pheasant breast with dried cherries, balsamic vinegar, and port wine sauce. The third-place finisher was Chef Mark Haugen, who served cardamom-cured venison steaks with venison confit tamale, black bean salsa, and cranberry-ancho chutney.

All of the finalists' dishes, however, were acclaimed by the judges. Judge John Folse, owner and executive chef of Lafitte's Landing in Louisiana, undoubtedly spoke for the entire panel when he said, "I have never judged a competition where the skill of the chefs was so prevalent. It was difficult judging one through five."

"The real significance of this event," Folse added, "is that these participants came from all over the country to this little town in the northwoods of Wisconsin because they wanted to prove that their cooking could stand up to the judgment of the professional culinary community."

It was an auspicious beginning, but preparations for the second annual competition began almost immediately.

In the second year, the amount of prize money offered was more than doubled; the competition again attracted over 100 entrants and some 150 recipes. Although the number of recipes had not increased, the caliber of those recipes rose dramatically. "The quality just doubled in one year—and the quality improved again in the third year," according to Chef Ray.

Finalists selected for the 1994 competition included Benjamin Bailey, sous chef at the Omni Hotel in Houston, Texas; Raul Lacara, chef at the Nob Hill Restaurant in San Francisco's Mark Hopkins Intercontinental Hotel; Michael Rork, executive chef at the Harbor Court Hotel in Baltimore; Gregory Werry, newly appointed executive chef at the Bellevue Athletic Club in Bellevue, Washington; and Jamie Boelhower, chef in the President's Room of the Milwaukee Athletic Club.

A special event held in conjunction with the 1994 competition was an "all-you-care-to-eat" wild game outdoor food festival, open to the public at $12.95 per adult. Festivalgoers met the celebrity chefs and were treated to sides of smoked salmon, bear chili, roast boar on a spit, barbecued venison, baron of buffalo, salads, grilled corn on the cob, and an array of products offered by sponsors of the competition. The feast was an attempt to get the local community involved. It was a rousing success for those who attended, but an all-day rain apparently discouraged many people. Over 100 folks turned out, but 500 had been expected.

The awards banquet that evening, prepared once again by Chef Ray and his staff, had been expanded from eight courses to nine. Highlights included arctic char, carpaccio of lamb, roast red bell pepper soup, maple-glazed venison chops, and smoked duck salad. The grand prize winner at the 1994 competition was Chef Greg Werry, who was awarded $2,500 for his preparation, an exquisite Thai-roasted venison with sesame shrimp, ginger barley pilaf, glazed shiitake spring roll, and long bean sauté.

It was another tough year for the judges, however. Raul Lacara garnered the second-place award of $1,000 for his delicious smoked and seared medallions of pheasant and venison loin with roasted red bell pepper oil and foie gras pudding, served with fresh mango chutney. Michael Rork took the $500 third prize by preparing braised, stuffed venison shanks with pheasant and champagne truffle risotto, served with red lentils and spring vegetables. Modestly, Chef Rork described his culinary creation as a "northwoods bistro plate."

"We became very legitimate in 1995," Chef Ray observes. "The first two years, I felt like a stepchild. We were getting press only as an afterthought. I pounded the media with press releases, and we'd get nothing."

Many things changed in 1995. For starters, the media began approaching Chef Ray, not the other way around—perhaps because he had proven that the Original National Wild Game Cooking Competition was here to stay.

In the interim, the chef had left Dun Rovin Lodge to accept a position as executive chef and partner at the Flat Creek Eatery and Saloon, a restaurant within the modern, newly opened Hayward Country Inn and Suites. The 1995 competition would be held at the inn, which boasts 65 rooms and 24 suites (eight equipped with whirlpools), and the Flat Creek Eatery was scheduled to open just four weeks prior to the competition. Chef Ray had to hire and train his restaurant staff (some of whom came from the local Hardee's), order supplies, and attend to all the grand opening details, in addition to coordinating the competition.

On the positive side, the kitchen in the new restaurant had been designed by Chef Ray and built to his specifications. It was a gleaming workspace dominated by stainless steel, larger and better-equipped than the kitchen at Dun Rovin. And the brand-new ballroom across the hall, where the 1995 awards banquet would be held, was a spacious, elegant room that would allow the chef and his staff to serve a bigger crowd.

Contest entries were slow to arrive in 1995. "We were nervous for five weeks," Chef Ray says. By March 10, the day before the entry deadline, only 60-some entries had been received, down significantly from previous years. "We were getting a lot of phone calls from chefs, but nobody was entering. I wondered, 'Are we losing our snap? Do we not have the pizazz we thought we had?'" However, a landslide of last-minute entries put the total over the 100 mark for the third year in a row, and the 1995 finalists were announced a week later.

For the first time since the competition began, one of the finalists was forced to cancel his appearance. Chef Andre Halston, then the executive chef at the Ritz-Carlton Hotel in Cleveland, called on Thursday, just two days before the cook-off. With profuse apologies, Halston told Chef Ray he had just left a corporate meeting. "I'm really sorry, but there's no way I can leave the property this weekend. We just fired four of my chefs."

To further complicate things, 1995 was also the first year that a judge was unable to attend. Greg Werry, the 1994 cooking competition winner, was slated to be the only chef among the judges for the '95 edition, but a family emergency forced him to cancel. On the Wednesday before the competition, Werry contacted Greg Taylor, an American Culinary Federation-approved judge and a chef who had himself won a gold medal in the International Culinary Olympics. Taylor agreed to serve as a replacement judge.

The judging problem appeared to be resolved, but Chef Ray was forced to scramble for a new finalist. After considering a number of alternatives, he asked Chef Greg Taylor to assume the fifth slot as a contestant, instead of serving as a judge. Given the short notice, Chef Taylor was reluctant at first, but he assented on Thursday afternoon—just eleven hours before he was scheduled to drive from his hometown of Portland to the Seattle airport, then fly to Minneapolis and drive on to Hayward. As it turned out, he was the first of the finalists to arrive on Friday, although he had not yet decided which recipe he would prepare for the competition. He had simply rounded up an assortment of his favorite ingredients and brought them all with him.

As for the judges, Chef Ray decided to go with a three-member panel, all of whom were knowledgeable food editors, although he ideally prefers to have at least one chef on the panel. Chefs, he says, "understand the complexities, textures, colors, and tastes. They know what goes into the preparation of a dish, and what the chef is trying to say to you on the plate."

During the days preceding the competition, Chef Ray also worked hard to convey the significance of the event to his new staff. A basketball metaphor proved the most effective. "It's like the Los Angeles Lakers were coming to play the Chicago Bulls in an exhibition here in the Hayward High School gym!" he told his staff. "We've got Michael Jordans and Magic Johnsons coming in here!"

Chef Greg Taylor assumes his natural role as an educator with a member of the Flat Creek staff.

Chef Ray arrived at work shortly before 8 a.m. on Saturday, April 22—the morning of the 1995 cook-off. There were no finalists in evidence, and their absence reflected the chefs' thorough advance preparation. One finalist, Master Chef Michael Robins, the director of culinary services for CPC Foodservice in Franklin Park, Illinois, would be serving cold-smoked quail during the cook-off. Robins, the youngest chef ever to become an American Culinary Federation-certified master chef in the United States, had won three gold medals at the World Culinary Olympics—including one gold medal with distinction for obtaining perfect scores. Before leaving Franklin Park, he had turned on his smoker, placed his quail pieces in freezer bags, used a hair dryer to blow smoke into the bags, and sealed each one. Thus, during his trip to Hayward, Robins' quail was "self-smoking."

Chef Guy Reinbolt, a native of Alsace, France who has trained with some of the top chefs in Europe, was the first finalist to venture into the kitchen. He immediately began preparations for his millefeuille, a multi-layered entree. Chef Reinbolt, the chef de cuisine of the Willard Room in Washington, D.C.'s Willard Intercontinental Hotel, was the picture of organized motion. Everything he did had an urgency of purpose—not surprising, since his millefeuille included layers of pounded elk, chestnut puree, Portobello mushrooms, and spinach and foie gras that were first tied, then seared, then baked before being garnished with Swiss cheese and heated briefly in the oven.

Chef Greg Taylor, still deciding which recipe he would prepare, arrived next, setting up his work zone at the end of what is normally the pizza and dessert preparation area. He was visible to customers in the restaurant, and his activities created a stir among guests of the inn who were there for a Saturday morning breakfast. As he prepared a mushroom stuffing for individual turkey servings and a sauce with tomatoes, morel mushrooms, pearl onions, and roasted garlic, a small but inquisitive audience gathered.

Anthony Robles was the next to appear. Chef Robles, who supervises a prep staff of about 15 people at Stephan Pyles' Star Canyon Restaurant in Dallas, Texas, evidenced a take-charge working style. Within minutes, two members of Chef Ray's staff had been recruited as his assistants; they were busily cleaning basil and performing chiffonade (rolling greens and cutting them so they come out shredded). Chef Robles had brought a photograph of his son Martin with him, and in fact named his creation "Martin the Dish" in tribute to his four-year-old boy.

The fourth finalist in the kitchen was Kerry Leigh Heffernan, chef de cuisine at the Sheraton Palace Hotel in San Francisco's Nob Hill District and the first female to be chosen as a finalist. Her air of professional confidence was apparent, despite the fact that she had never before appeared in a cooking competition. She talked with the reporters and admirers from the Hayward area who had begun to crowd into the kitchen area as she sliced strips of wild boar bacon from a slab and wrapped previously boned and marinated quail in the bacon. For her competition entry, she combined the bacon-wrapped quail with warm salad, truffled foie gras croutons, and pinot noir sauce.

The fifth finalist to appear was Chef Michael Robins, who brought with him a 5x7 color photograph of the plate that he was about to prepare. Robins was entirely at ease with a radio interviewer, cameras, and questions from reporters—perhaps because he had cooked around cables, lights, and microphones as part of his training for the World Culinary Olympics.

The cook-off itself began shortly after noon. Now the chefs put their recipes—and their professionalism—on the line. Chef Robles' dish, a bison strip loin marinated in ancho chili paste, garnished with an apple and fig au jus, and served with an orange-cinnamon couscous tart filled with a savory custard, was presented first to the judges by Chef Ray. The chefs themselves are not allowed to be in the room while the judges sample their culinary creations.

The 1995 judges were Brad Johnson, associate food editor from *Restaurants and Institutions* magazine; Sue Zellickson, food reporter for WCCO/CBS Radio; and Lee Aschoff, food editor and restaurant critic from the *Milwaukee Journal-Sentinel*. They were to evaluate the finalists' entries based on the following criteria: up to 50 points on taste, 30 points on

Carl Nordberg talks things over with Anthony Robles.

presentation, and 20 points on originality. The winner, obviously, would be the chef with the highest score.

Once again, it was an extraordinarily close match. At the judges' request, Chef Ray spent half an hour behind closed doors in the ballroom, impartially answering questions from the judges about the finalists' dishes. When it was all over, an average of just 1.3 points separated the second, third, and fourth-place finishers. However, the results would not be announced for another six or seven hours. The competing chefs had more work to do, as did Chef Ray and his staff.

The special feature of the 1995 competition was a cooking seminar conducted by the five finalists and open to the public. Each chef performed a half-hour "demo," during which he or she prepared the cook-off recipe once again. Sponsors of the competition were mentioned prominently, and Berndes SilverStone cookware representatives benefitted from the spectacle of their pots and pans withstanding the flames that were shooting out from some of the chefs' preparations. The demos, says Chef Ray, are "part of giving something back to Hayward. We're giving knowledge and a free professional performance to the community."

More than 200 people turned out for the cooking seminars, and they all received a copy of the finalists' recipes. Sponsor products were available for sampling without charge. The chefs thoroughly enjoyed themselves. For some of them, it was a rare instance of public recognition for an art that takes place primarily behind kitchen doors and out of sight of the dining public.

The demos began at 2 p.m. and were slated to conclude at 4:30. However, every session ran long, due to questions from dazzled spectators. Sometime after 5:30, a delighted Chef Ray diplomatically asked the final chef to wrap up his presentation. Dinner was scheduled to start in an hour, and the demo section of the ballroom had to be set up with tables, chairs, tablecloths, and place settings. Then the awards banquet, the crowning production of the 1995 competition, would begin.

For the $75 per plate banquet, the chefs were seated at separate tables—an arrangement that allowed them to mingle with many of the diners. The affair required jackets but not ties, in deference to the casual northwoods lifestyle.

Few people outside of the food industry realize the amount of planning, coordination, drama, anxiety, intensity, and just plain perspiration that goes into the staging of a multi-course banquet. Chef Ray and his staff had been putting in long hours for several days, preparing portions of the nine-course banquet in advance. If the expected 200 people attended the banquet, the newly trained Flat Creek staff would serve 1,800 "plates" over the course of the evening—an accomplishment that would intimidate far larger and more experienced staffs. What follows is a behind the scenes look at the 1995 banquet:

The evening marathon begins at about 6:45.

"We've already lined five people up at our two stainless tables (in the kitchen), and those people do not leave their spots for over two-and-a-half hours," Chef Ray says. "I'm getting crazy about now."

Presentation of dinner by the waitstaff is on a rigid schedule: set at 6:45, clear at 6:55, pour wine at 7:00, set at 7:05, clear at 7:15, and so on. A kind of militarized madness prevails throughout the evening, but here's the key: None of the diners feel as if they're being rushed, and there's no sign of anxiety among members of the waitstaff. These are hallmarks of a first-class banquet.

Back in the kitchen, where the temperature is rising, Chef Ray is a blur—coordinating, tasting, cooking, and directing his fellow chefs. As the dishes and trays from one course come back, another course is transported to the banquet hall—and there are logistics to overcome. One of the hot courses must be served on plates that do not fit in the restaurant's hot carts, so the plates are stacked on trays and Sterno-fueled candles are used to keep them warm.

The first course, a smoked salmon cheesecake, has been pre-plated with a sauce of blueberries and strawberries. However, the accompanying wheat wafers could not be pre-plated because they would get soggy in the cooler. So the kitchen staff labors to place three crackers on each plate before it goes out.

The staff members have begun to settle into a rhythm, and they're keenly aware that Chef Ray expects nothing short of total concentration from employees. "They know I can be a maniac at times," says Chef Ray. "They don't want to get me screaming and yelling, but in this sort of situation I would never do that to them." The smoked salmon cheesecake, which resembles a paté rather than a dessert, turns out to be one of the evening's biggest hits, and it's complemented by a four-ounce pour of Schmaltz Alt, an August Schell product with a dark cast and a slightly sweet flavor.

Course number two is peppered, pan-seared tilapia, served on wheat berry ragout and garnished with a red onion and port wine compote. Tilapia, Chef Ray explains, is a fish native to South Africa. It has a taste similar to crappie, with a texture somewhere between walleye and perch. The tilapia is cooked quickly at high heat; then a kitchen employee scoops the fish up and adds the hot wheat berry ragout; another person adds scallions, and still another is in charge of the port onion compote, which consists of red onions cooked thoroughly in port wine. Another employee organizes and empties incoming trays, while the waitstaff enters the kitchen just long enough to grab trays loaded with the next course. "It's a fiasco," Chef Ray admits. "But it's an organized fiasco."

The third course is a carpaccio of (raw) lamb on a mint pesto sauce, garnished with tomato concasse and chili pepper olive oil. The mint pesto sauce had been pre-plated, but the staff was not able to slice the lamb until 3 p.m. that day, because it would discolor if sliced too early. The lamb is served with tomato blanched in water and peeled, and a drizzle of the chili pepper olive oil is added atop the meat. Two people are engaged in putting the course on the waitstaff's trays.

Course number four is a true wild game confection—oven-roasted quail, filled with bear forcemeat and served on a three-bean salad. The restaurant does not have a sufficient number of trays or carts to pre-plate the three-bean salad, so the staff is engaged in doing so. "Now we're plating cold food, which we didn't want to do," Chef Ray notes. Each portion of quail is hand-split with a knife, so it will appear on the plate just the way Chef Ray intended. Meanwhile the next course—Indian pumpkin soup—is already hot, and its sequel, a palate-cleansing melon sorbet, is also ready.

At this point, perhaps an hour into the banquet, the kitchen staff is flagging, and things are threatening to back up. Three dishwashers strain to keep up with the load of dirty dishes and trays that seem to bounce back like malicious boomerangs from the banquet hall. "I'm dealing with an exhausted crew right now, and it's my job to keep them up, keep them going. Everyone is dripping sweat, and we still have a lot of things to do," Chef Ray says.

His strategy? "I start singing—rap, reggae, blues, opera—whatever I think I'm good at that day. They know that if we're doing a banquet and I'm singing, we must be doing great."

Then he adds a few words of genuine enthusiasm. "Have you ever had more fun? This is fantastic!"

And finally, a warning. "We've got hell ahead of us. Our hardest presentation is coming up."

That challenge is neither the Indian pumpkin soup nor the melon sorbet, both of which are a comparative breeze—although a splash of spiced rum and a slice of lime must be added to each cup of sorbet as it makes its way out the door.

Nor is the hardest presentation course number seven, a filet of salmon braised and served in a shrimp/tomato broth with mustard greens. The entire course must be cooked on the spot. The greens are heated carefully, in a manner that eliminates bitterness while maintaining the color. The salmon is cooked at the same time, and one filet is added to each small pile of greens on the plate. Before the course is ready to depart the kitchen, just the right amount of broth is poured into each dish.

Midway through the salmon, the cooks sag. The pace drops, and Chef Ray again intervenes. "We're moving like snails!" he hollers to the staff. "You'd think you guys were tired or something. Well, I've got good news for you. The hardest course is next." However, the chef is not worried. He knows what time it is, and the operation is, miraculously, running slightly ahead of schedule.

Athena Dedrick, a staff member at the Flat Creek Eatery, prepares for the awards banquet.

The dreaded "hardest course" is a smoked wild boar salad, which must be tossed, assembled, and garnished on the spot. The boar is served on a paper-thin Greek pastry flavored with a subtle hint of walnut, but three chefs had painstakingly created these pastry shells earlier in the week. The tossed salad is artfully placed inside the pastry shells. Pieces of smoked boar are carefully fanned out on the salad. A drizzle of vinaigrette is added atop the meat. Then the dish is completed with a garnish of roast pecans. Only three or four of these plates fit on a tray, so service in the ballroom requires more than the usual number of back and forth excursions on the part of the waitstaff.

Then, abruptly, it's over—at least as far as Chef Ray is concerned. Dessert is a northwoods wild rice cake pre-made by Lady Dianne Gourmet Desserts, a competition sponsor. With a final hurrah of encouragement to his beleaguered staff, Chef Ray leaves the kitchen, changes out of his stained chef's jacket, dons a suitcoat, and strolls into the banquet hall. He takes a chair next to his wife, Karen, as the diners finish their wild boar salad. The time is about 9:30.

1995 winners, from left to right: Kerry Leigh Heffernan, Third Prize; Michael Robins, Second Prize and Creativity Award, Anthony Robles, Grand Prize, and competition organizer, Christopher Ray, with the famed "Chef Pig."

"I'm ruthless," Chef Ray says with a smile. "I make the finalists eat nine courses before they find out how the awards came out."

During the banquet, the tireless Carl Nordberg has served as toastmaster, displaying his own considerable knowledge of cuisine by introducing and explaining each course as it arrives. Now, though, it's time to energize the chef who planned and engineered the evening. Chef Ray's adrenaline is beginning to subside, so Nordberg performs much the same role for Chef Ray that the chef played earlier for his kitchen staff. Taking him aside for a moment, Nordberg tells Chef Ray, "I just want you to know this was the best piece of work you've ever done in your career."

The diners have been seated for nearly three hours, so it's time to move the proceedings along. Nordberg begins the awards announcements by publicly introducing Chef Ray, who receives a standing ovation led by the five finalists. Nordberg presents Chef Ray with "the biggest prize of the night," a two-foot-tall, ceramic "chef pig" sporting a chef's hat and jacket and wielding a wooden fork and spoon. The practice of awarding chef pigs originated in Europe, and receiving one is considered a high honor. Today, that chef pig stands proudly on the front counter of the Flat Creek Eatery's kitchen, a symbol of the restaurant's culinary aspirations.

Chef Ray introduces his entire staff, which has now served dessert and Australian Skybury coffee, provided by a locally based competition sponsor, Cameron's Coffee Company. Chef Ray notes that all of the employees are from the Hayward area, and he credits them with doing the bulk of the work. The crowd applauds vigorously, providing the staff members with their moment of well-deserved acclaim. The chef also presents a special plaque to Nordberg, lauding him for his years of service to the cooking competition.

Two consolation prizes of $250 are awarded to Chefs Greg Taylor and Guy Reinbolt. Chef Michael Robins receives a special $250 creativity award, then third prize is awarded to Chef Kerry Leigh Heffernan. Chef Robins also receives the $1,000 second prize, which removes all doubt concerning the identity of the 1995 grand prize winner. The award is presented by Chef Ray and the restaurant's managing partner, Dave Weber.

In his acceptance speech, Chef Anthony Robles calls winning the competition "a great honor." He tells the audience that he is a self-taught chef who began working in professional kitchens as a child, alongside his mother at a cafe in the Oklahoma City stockyards. Chef Robles confesses that he has been going through trying times lately—his wife divorced him a year ago, against his wishes. He explains how seriously he takes his responsibilities as a father, and how important his family is to him. Chef Robles announces that he will use the $2,500 prize money to take a vacation with his son Martin, who "means the world to me." There are more than a few moist eyes in the house as a most memorable banquet comes to its conclusion.

Looking back to late 1992, Chef Ray recalls the first challenge he faced: defining the format and purpose of the cooking competition. He had participated in a number of cook-offs during his career, and some were less than pleasant experiences. He had encountered shabby treatment of the chefs, plus an atmosphere of "cutthroat competition" that encouraged hostility rather than professional camaraderie. Chef Ray was determined to avoid the mistakes he'd seen at other competitions. "It's what you learn not to do sometimes that's important," he says.

His primary model for the first National Wild Game Cooking Competition was a superbly orchestrated, one-year-only competition called Pasta Power, held in California and put on by Radisson International Hotels. The three finalists, including Chef Ray, were "treated like kings." They were flown to a sponsoring winery. They then spent three days together, touring the redwoods, trading culinary stories, and becoming fast friends. "By the time we got into the kitchen, everyone was friendly and cordial," Chef Ray recalls. "There was still a competitive edge, but you were happy to see someone win, even if it wasn't you."

He finished second in this national competition—an impressive achievement—but the most valuable thing he learned was how to conduct a first-class cooking competition. He learned similar lessons while competing in A Taste of Elegance, a first-class cook-off sponsored annually by the Pork Producers Council.

The overriding purpose of the Original National Wild Game Cooking Competition, Chef Ray decided, would be to celebrate great chefs and their culinary accomplishments, and perhaps to learn techniques and practices from them during their weekend in Hayward.

Today, Chef Ray feels he has remained true to that mission. "I wanted to bring chefs up to the northwoods to get to know each other. I wanted to keep contestants happy, develop camaraderie, send them Christmas cards, call them up, send letters, and keep the relationships going. That we have definitely accomplished. There's no two ways about it."

Plans for 1996 include bringing the grand prize winners from the first three competitions back as judges, and holding a special "champion of champions" cook-off between them at a Friday night reception. The extra competitive element may enhance the public's awareness of this unique celebration of wild game cuisine. "Right now," Chef Ray says, "the competition is a big event within the trade. I want to make it a big event in the public's eyes, too." The cooking demonstrations will return, and a second edition of *The Wild Menu* will be published, including the winning recipes from the 1996 competition and many more of the best recipes submitted.

There's a saying that was handed down to Chef Ray by his father, a treasured piece of advice that he often thinks about: "An overnight success takes 20 years." By this standard, the "overnight success" fostered by Chef Ray, Carl Nordberg, and all of the participants in the Original National Wild Game Cooking Competition is running years ahead of schedule.

Chef Profiles: The 1995 Finalists

Chef Anthony R. Robles
GRAND PRIZE WINNER

Chef Robles began his culinary career at a cafe in the Oklahoma City stockyards where, as a child, he worked in the kitchen alongside his mother. Self-taught, he now serves as sous chef at the acclaimed Star Canyon Restaurant in Dallas, Texas, where chef and owner Stephan Pyles offers "new Texas cuisine." In 1995, Star Canyon received a James Beard nomination for the Milliken Best New Restaurant Award, marking it as one of the most outstanding new restaurants in the United States.

Chef Robles is particularly talented in the preparation and presentation of seafoods, meats, and soups. He is a certified food service manager and an active member of the American Culinary Federation, and he previously worked with Chef Pyles at the renowned Baby Routh restaurant in Texas. He has also served as head chef and sous chef at the Montrachet Bistro in Tulsa, Oklahoma.

Bison Strip with Ancho Chile Rub, Couscous Tart Crust, and Apple Custard

Chef Michael Robins
SECOND PRIZE AND CREATIVITY AWARD WINNER

Chef Robins is the youngest American to achieve the status of Certified Master Chef, awarded by the American Culinary Federation's Education Institute. He is a graduate with honors of the prestigious Culinary Institute of America, and he now serves as director of culinary services for CPC International, a Fortune 100 food manufacturing company known for such brand names as Knorr, Best Foods, Mazola, Skippy, Hellmann's, and Brownberry. He is a contributing author to *The Art and Science of Culinary Preparation*, a textbook used by culinary apprenticeship programs throughout the United States.

Chef Robins has received three gold medals at the World Culinary Olympics, including a gold medal with distinction for perfect scores. He has won two gold medals at the American Seafood Challenge competition, and in 1993 he was named Grand Champion at The National Game and Game Fish Cook-off.

Prior to assuming his current position, Chef Robins served as corporate executive chef for Sunbelt Hospitality in North Carolina, a Hilton management company. He is an active member of the American Culinary Federation, the Chain Des Rotisseurs, and the Institute of Food Technologists.

Smoked Field-Style Quail with Lentils, Apple and Red Onion Confit, and Sweet Wild Rice and Corn Pudding

Chef Kerry Leigh Heffernan
THIRD PRIZE WINNER

Born and raised in southern California, Chef Heffernan became interested in complex cooking at an early age, perhaps because cooking was part of her family heritage. Her maternal grandmother served as a chef in the homes of several Hollywood celebrities during the 1940s and 1950s, and her great-grandmother owned an Italian restaurant in Rhode Island at the turn of the century.

As the chef de cuisine for the Garden Court of the Sheraton Palace Hotel, located in San Francisco's Nob Hill District, Chef Heffernan oversees all aspects of the lunch and dinner menus. Prior to her current position, she served as the executive sous chef of Elka, considered by many to be the most innovative seafood restaurant in the western United States.

Earlier in her career, Chef Heffernan served an apprenticeship at the world-renowned Beverly Hills Hotel, worked at the corporate headquarters of the Ritz-Carlton in Atlanta, Georgia, and subsequently returned to Los Angeles as a sous chef to open the Checkers Hotel. In San Francisco, she has also served as sous chef of the Cypress Club and executive chef of the Paragon restaurant.

Wild Boar Bacon-Wrapped Quail with Warm Salad, Truffled Foie Gras Croutons, and Pinot Noir Sauce

Chef Guy Reinbolt
CONSOLATION AWARD WINNER

Chef Reinbolt is a native of Alsace, France, whose study of classic French cuisine led to the receipt of two prestigious degrees: the Bret D'Etude (BET), and the Certificat D'Aptitute Professionale (CAP), awarded by the Lycee D'Enseigment Professionale et Hotellier de Guebwiller. He currently serves as chef de cuisine of the Willard Room in Washington D.C.'s Willard Inter-Continental Hotel.

After working in both Germany and France, Chef Reinbolt moved to New Orleans in 1990, where he served as executive sous chef at La Gauloise and Henri, both restaurants within the Hotel Meridien. He then moved to Memphis, Tennessee, and the renowned Chez Philippe restaurant in the Peabody Hotel.

At the Willard Room, Chef Reinbolt offers a blend of classic cuisine presented in the modern style with nouvelle cuisine, drawing upon his international experience and his extensive culinary knowledge.

Millefeuille of Elk Saddle and Foie Gras with Roasted Bengalines of Pheasant and Perigourdine Sauce

Chef Greg A. Taylor
1995 CONSOLATION AWARD WINNER

Chef Taylor is a chef instructor at the Western Culinary Institute in Portland, Oregon. He is also executive director of L'Art de Cuisine International, a culinary consulting and educational enterprise. In the past, he has served as executive chef of the Portland Golf Club, the Windmill Inn, and the Corvallis Country Club. He remains a C.W.C., or certified working chef.

Chef Taylor has won a number of awards in international competitions. At the 1992 International Culinary Olympics, held in Frankfurt, Germany, he received two gold medals, one silver medal, and two bronze medals in recognition of his cooking excellence. He won a gold and a silver medal at the 1990 Pacific Rim Grand Culinary Salon in Canada, and in 1994 took the grand prize at the United Grocers Hot Food Cook-off. Chef Taylor is also an American Culinary Federation-certified judge, which entitles him to evaluate the work of his chef colleagues at cook-offs and competitions.

Smoked Wild Turkey Cotelettes with Wild Boar Bacon, Wild Watercress Sauce, Kiln-Dried Cherry Chutney, Braised Cattail Shoots, Fiddlehead Ferns with Morels, Potato and Parsnip Cakes, and Onion Crispies

THE WILD MENU

Wild Game Recipes: You're the Chef

by Executive Chef Christopher P. Ray, Founder, The National Wild Game Cooking Competition

The most common and unfortunate misconception people have about cookbooks—especially chefs' cookbooks—is that every recipe should be prepared exactly as it appears. That's not the case!

I view a recipe as nothing more than a list of suggestions. Flexibility is my stock in trade, because the chef's life is one of improvisation. We're always making last-minute decisions that affect recipes. If a sauce isn't working, we change it. If a product is spoiled, we have to find a substitute. If a supplier forgets to deliver the rabbit loin we're scheduled to serve ten people at an elegant dinner, we have to prepare something else. In other words, we ad lib all the time, so don't be afraid to do the same. After all, you're the chef in your own kitchen!

You needn't rule a recipe out just because it includes an ingredient or two that you're not fond of. Let's suppose a recipe calls for figs, but you're not a fig fan. Feel free to substitute an ingredient you prefer—raisins, for instance. Suppose you're preparing a vegetable medley and the recipe calls for rosemary. You may feel that rosemary is too strong, or it may not be available in your kitchen. No problem! Use parsley or salt and pepper instead—or use no seasonings at all. For that matter, you can even change or eliminate some of the vegetables if that's your preference.

If you're in the mood for herbed white rice instead of the wild rice a recipe calls for, indulge yourself. If you don't like onions in lasagna, you can leave them out. My point is obvious by now, but I want to accomplish two things: I want to encourage your creativity; and I want you to feel that any recipe in *The Wild Menu* can be adapted to your needs or taste preferences.

The same goes for cooking techniques. If a recipe asks you to create elements from scratch, you can enjoy the satisfaction that comes from doing so, but there may be another option. You may be able to buy some items premade from a grocery store or purchase special cuts of meat from a butcher shop, for example.

Some of our recipes consist of an entree with an accompanying sauce. Other recipes have multiple parts, offering tasty and compatible accompaniments such as relishes, salads, starches, or vegetables. Here again, you have a choice. Suppose a venison recipe includes a wild rice crepe to accompany it. Perhaps you've never made a crepe in your life, and today is not the day you want to begin your career as a crepe chef. By all means, make the venison by itself, and save the crepe for another occasion.

Remember that you can use *The Wild Menu* as a reference for more than meat dishes. For example, many of the delicious dressings or vinaigrettes we've included can add an exciting new dimension to your nightly dinner salad. Here again, substitution of ingredients is perfectly permissible. If you're not familiar with the sun-dried fruits you find in a vinaigrette recipe, substitute the fresh product or, if the ingredient lends itself to freezing, use the frozen product. For example, you might use frozen blueberries instead of fresh or sun-dried berries.

When you begin cooking, be sure to read the entire recipe so you understand it, but then break the recipe down, step by step. You'll find that even the more complicated recipes are easy if you approach them in this manner.

Don't be intimidated by unusual ingredients such as foie gras (goose liver). This delicacy is much easier to deal with than you might think—and don't feel you have to incorporate it if you don't want to.

Certain terms used by our chefs might seem mystifying, but most of them describe familiar concepts. "Mousseline," for example, is simply a filling of sorts. Don't let these words scare you away.

Here's a tip that may help you avoid much disappointment: *Never overcook wild game.* The heat needed to cook most wild game is not as intense or prolonged as the heat you would use in preparing beef and pork products. Wild game meats are lean and healthy. Most don't contain much fat or marbling—that's partly why you're cooking them!

When working with wild game, you can seal in the juices by first searing (browning) the meat briefly at very high heat, then finishing it in the oven. You'll find this technique recommended often in our recipes, because it ensures juicy, flavorful results. Another common approach to preparing wild game involves cooking it "low and slow"—using low heat and cooking the meat slowly. This way, the meat roasts in own juices, especially if you periodically baste it.

Many people are intimidated simply because a meat is unfamiliar—elk rather than beef, for example, or partridge rather than chicken. Don't hesitate to try different meats. Pull them out of your freezer just as you would any other meat, follow the basic preparation instructions, and enjoy a delicious meal!

The fact that a recipe is designed by a leading chef doesn't mean you can't understand it and recreate the recipe at home. In fact, the best chefs often create the most straightforward recipes.

We've tried to enhance the accessibility of our recipes in a number of ways. We've included "For Simplicity's Sake" sidebars with most recipes. These offer comments on recipes; tips on preparation and where to obtain ingredients; acceptable substitutions; explanations of terms and techniques; recipes for basic stocks and sauces; and much more. We hope they will answer most of your questions.

We've also included an extensive glossary with definitions, ranging once again from preparation techniques to names of dishes and ingredients. If you're stuck, be sure to check the glossary. Our "Basic Recipes" section includes directions for preparing a number of the basic sauces and accompanying dishes that are essential to our chefs' recipes. And finally, we offer a list of retailers and wholesalers from whom farm- or ranch-raised wild game can be obtained. Don't hesitate to contact any of these purveyors for further information.

As a professional chef, I always strive for excellence and quality. I attempt to use nothing but the finest, freshest ingredients available to me, but I realize that difficulties may be encountered when you're trying to recreate recipes in a home kitchen. We've tried to anticipate and help you resolve those difficulties.

There's a great degree of satisfaction and reward involved in combining all the accompaniments with a chef's entree, thereby recreating the blend of flavors and textures envisioned by the chef. However, the young, innovative chefs who champion wild game cuisine will be the first to tell you that the fundamental ingredient of every great recipe is the chef's own creativity.

Consider that your invitation to *The Wild Menu*. Be creative. Have fun. Enjoy a host of new eating experiences.

In other words, go wild!

The Finalists' Recipes

Bison Strip with Ancho Chile Rub
served with Couscous Tart Crust, and Apple Custard

Prepared by Anthony R. Robles, Sous Chef • Star Canyon Restaurant • Dallas, Texas   *Serves Four*

Bison Strip with Ancho Chile Rub

4 6-ounce bison strip loins

¼ cup ancho chile powder (or ½ cup ancho chile paste)

salt to taste

■ Marinate strip loins in ancho chile powder or paste for one hour. Add salt to taste. Accompany with couscous tart (below). To prepare the bison, sear the strip loins, then cook them in a 350° oven until medium rare (internal temperature of 120 degrees). Remove and let them rest before serving. The loins can be sliced or served in whole pieces.

To serve: Place tart in center of plate. Fan strip loin slices around the tart or place the whole loin on the plate. Add a generous portion of jus, so dried fruits garnish the plate. Grilled peppers and onions provide a nice accompaniment.

Couscous Tart Crust

1¼ cups couscous

2½ cups chicken stock

4 oranges, juice of

2 oranges, zest of (minced)

¼ tsp salt

1 bay leaf

1 cinnamon stick

1 tbsp butter

2 tbsp honey

1 egg white

1 whole egg

¼ cup masa harina (or all-purpose flour)

■ Cook the couscous in chicken stock with the orange juice, orange zest, salt, bay leaf, and cinnamon stick. Add butter and honey. Set aside to cool. When cool, add egg white, whole egg, and masa harina. Form the crust in miniature tart pans.

Custard

2 cups heavy cream

½ cup roasted walnuts

1 tbsp roasted garlic

pinch cayenne pepper

½ tsp kosher salt

2 fresh or dried figs, sliced

■ Reduce cream by half. Mix remaining ingredients in a mixing bowl. Garnish custard with apples and fresh or dried figs. Fill the tart pans with custard and bake in a 275° oven until firm. Remove from oven and let cool.

Jus

1 quart apple juice

¾ cup brandy

1 cup pearl onions

6 garlic cloves, chopped

3 cups apples, chopped

4 large shallots, chopped

3 sprigs thyme

■ Add all ingredients to a sauce pan and reduce by half.

Smoked Field-Style Quail with Lentils, Apple and Red Onion Confit, and Sweet Wild Rice and Corn Pudding

Prepared by Michael Robins, C.M.C. • CPC Foods • Chicago, Illinois   *Serves Four*

4 quail

salt and black pepper to taste

4 bunches wild greens (escarole, kale, chard)

1 cup apple vinaigrette

20 apple slices

½ red onion, sliced

1½ cups apple cider

¼ pound lentils

1 cup chicken stock

1½ cups mirepoix, diced

¼ cup red wine

1 cup demi-glace

¼ cup wild rice, cooked

½ cup cornbread, cooked

honey to taste

⅛ cup red pepper, diced

⅛ cup green pepper, diced

1 tbsp parsley, chopped

■ Clean quail by removing breast meat from carcass. Then remove leg and thigh section and thigh bone. Season the leg section with salt and pepper and hot-smoke (see "Basic Recipes" for procedure) until done. Keep warm.

■ Prepare apple and red onion confit by reducing apple cider until thick. Add red onions and simmer until onions are tender. Cook lentils in stock with mirepoix, red wine, and demi-glaze.

■ Prepare wild rice and corn pudding by combining crumbled cornbread with cooked wild rice, honey, and sautéd peppers. Finish with chopped parsley.

■ Just prior to serving, season the quail breast with salt and pepper and sauté on high heat.

To serve: Arrange smoked quail and quail breast on a bed of salad greens. Place cooked lentils under quail breast. Garnish plate with corn pudding, confit, and apple slices. Sprinkle vinaigrette on salad greens.

Wild Boar Bacon-Wrapped Quail
with Warm Salad, Truffled Foie Gras Croutons, and Pinot Noir Sauce

Prepared by Kerry Leigh Heffernan, Chef de Cuisine • *Sheraton Palace Hotel* • *San Francisco*   *Serves Four*

Wild Boar Bacon-Wrapped Quail and Warm Salad

1 marinated boneless quail, wrapped with wild boar bacon
1½ cups braising greens (escarole, kale, chard)
½ cup savoy cabbage, julienned
1 tbsp rosemary oil
2 ½-ounce slices, foie gras
½ tsp truffle shavings
2 tbsp butter
1 tbsp pure olive oil
2 sourdough croutons, sliced on the bias
1 sprig fried rosemary
1½ ounces pinot noir sauce

■ Sear the quail to rare in the olive oil, then set aside to rest. Sauté the spicy braising greens and savoy cabbage with the butter, and set aside to drain. In a smoking hot pan, sear the foie gras. Place it on the croutons and top with truffle shavings. Place sautéed greens in the middle of the plate, with the croutons poking out from underneath like rabbit ears. While arranging the plate, put the quail in a hot oven and finish cooking to medium rare (120° internal). Remove quail from oven and slice in half through the breast. To prepare fried rosemary, fry a sprig in hot oil for 20 to 30 seconds.

Marinade

10 lemons, zest of
1 bunch rosemary, unchopped
1 tbsp fresh ground black pepper
20 peeled garlic cloves, unchopped
4 cups duck fat (or olive oil)

Rosemary Oil

3 bunches rosemary, blanched and shocked
3 bunches Italian parsley, blanched and shocked
1 bunch chives, blanched and shocked
4 cups canola oil

■ Squeeze the water from the herbs, then chop roughly and place in large blender. Add canola oil and blend for five minutes. Strain overnight through a fine cheesecloth, without disrupting or forcing the mixture through the cloth. Store in clear plastic squeeze bottle with a tight-fitting lid.

Pinot Noir Sauce

1 bottle pinot noir
4 pounds roasted game bones (rabbit, duck, quail, squab)
½ gallon veal stock (or chicken stock)
½ pound shallots, chopped
½ pound carrots, chopped
¼ pound mushroom stems
pinch black peppercorns
pinch butter

■ Sweat the shallots, carrots, mushroom stems, and peppercorns in a large stock pot. Roast the bones in a hot oven until browned, then add the bones to the stock pot. Pour the wine over the vegetables and bones and reduce by half. Pour the stock in the pot and reduce by half. Strain. To serve, bring the sauce to a boil and season to taste, adding butter to smooth the sauce.

To serve: Place the greens on the plate, and criss-cross the quail on top of the greens. Drizzle the plate with rosemary oil and pinot noir sauce, and garnish with fried rosemary.

Millefeuille of Elk Saddle and Foie Gras
with Roasted Bengalines of Pheasant and Perigourdine Sauce

Prepared by Guy Reinbolt, Chef de Cuisine • Willard Intercontinental Hotel • Washington, D.C.　　　*Serves Four*

Millefeuille

1 elk saddle loin, cleaned and
　trimmed
2 bunches large leaf spinach
2 pounds whole chestnuts
1 can chestnut puree
1 quart heavy cream
4 shallots
2 potatoes
2 pounds large portobello
　mushrooms
1 pound foie gras
1¾ ounces Swiss cheese

The pre-cleaned and trimmed elk saddle can be ordered from your butcher. Pound the elk with a meat hammer until thin, then refrigerate. Chop the whole chestnuts and shallots and sweat them (see glossary). Add one cup of cream and half can of chestnut puree. Reduce the liquid, then add salt and pepper. Roast the portobello mushrooms and dry them on a paper towel. Steam the potatoes with the remaining chestnut puree. When cooked, blend both the potatoes and puree. Blanch the spinach. Take a thin layer of elk saddle, cover it with a layer of spinach, cover with a slice of foie gras, add another layer of spinach, and a layer of the chestnut-shallot mix. Repeat the process once more, then tie everything together and refrigerate.

Bengalines

1 pheasant
1 carrot
2 zucchinis
2 onions
2 turnips
1 bunch celery
1 pound shiitake mushrooms
2 cups heavy cream
1 leek
6 sheets brick paper
salt and pepper to taste
2 pounds butter
2 cups white wine
1 loaf white bread, unsliced
dash cognac
dash porto

Roast the whole pheasant, maintaining a medium rare (120°) temperature, then debone it. Cut the pheasant into small dices. Cut a brunoise (very small dice) of carrots, shiitake mushrooms, leek, celery, and onion. Sweat the vegetables together, then add white wine and reduce. Add one cup of heavy cream and reduce again. Add diced pheasant and cook for five minutes, then let cool. When cool, wrap the pheasant mix in brick paper and make into an egg shape. Refrigerate.

Garniture

1 head frisee lettuce
1 head red oak lettuce
6 bouquets mache salad

Sauce

pheasant bones
elk bones
mirepoix of vegetables
⅛ to ¼ cup truffle
½ ounce tomato paste
⅛ cup flour
1 cup white wine

To prepare sauce, roast the bones of both the elk saddle and the pheasant. Then add the mirepoix, letting them sweat. Slowly add flour and tomato paste, and cook for two minutes. Add wine and water, and cook slowly for two hours.

■ Cut the loaf of white bread into large croutons and toast them to a golden brown. Devein the foie gras and mix it with soft butter, cognac, porto (port wine), salt, and pepper. Spread a layer over each crouton and refrigerate. Slice the truffle into 12 slices, then chop the rest and set aside. Strain the stock and reduce by half, then add one cup of cream and reduce. Add remaining foie gras trimmings, blend together, strain, and set aside. Cut a marienere of carrots, zucchinis, and turnips. Blanch them separately and let them cool, then set aside. Whip two cups heavy cream. Clean the greens and make six nice bouquets.

■ To finish, sear the millefeuille, then cook in a 450° oven for five minutes until it is a medium temperature. Roast the bengalines to a golden brown. Remove the millefeuille from the oven and slice. Cover with Swiss cheese slices and gratinee (brown). Remove the croutons from the refrigerator and place two bengalines on each crouton, then heat them briefly in the oven. Take half of the chestnut mousseline and heat. Add two teaspoons of whipped cream when hot. Spoon the mousseline and cream mixture onto the plate. Place millefeuille on top of the mixture. Place the bengaline crouton next to the millefeuille. Spoon sauce around the millefeuille and crouton. Heat the mariniere of vegetables with butter and sprinkle on plate. Stand a bouquet of greens in each mouselline.

Smoked Wild Turkey Cotelettes

with Wild Boar Bacon, Wild Watercress Sauce, Kiln-Dried Cherry Chutney, Braised Cattail Shoots, Fiddlehead Ferns with Morels, Potato and Parsnip Cakes, and Onion Crispies

Prepared by Greg Taylor, C.W.C. • Chef Instructor, Western Culinary Institute • Portland, Oregon   *Serves Four*

Smoked Wild Turkey Cotelettes

4 ¼-pound wild turkey breasts, sliced and pounded

2 caul fat sheets

2 rashers wild boar bacon

1 tbsp butter

1 pound wild mushrooms

2 tbsp garlic

2 tbsp shallots

2 tbsp parsley

1 tbsp thyme

1 tsp salt

1 tsp black pepper

2 egg whites

½ pound wild turkey leg meat, fine minced or ground

■ Begin by rough-chopping the mushrooms. Then pre-heat a sauté pan and add the butter, but do not burn. Add shallots and cook until translucent. Add garlic and chopped mushrooms. Sauté the mushroom mixture until soft, then place mixture in a strainer and allow liquid to run off. Set this mushroom essence aside for the sauce. Allow the mixture to cool, then add the balance of the herbs and spices. Fold in the turkey leg meat and the egg whites.

■ Pound the turkey breast slices between two sheets of plastic wrap, making sure the breasts are large enough to stuff. Add the stuffing mixture and fold in the corners. Wrap with caul fat, which can be requested from your butcher. Top with two rashers of wild boar bacon. Hot-smoke the turkey cotelettes with apple or pear wood, or with your favorite smoking chips.

Wild Watercress Sauce

1 bunch wild watercress

1 garlic clove

1 cup extra virgin olive oil

1 tsp salt

1 tsp cayenne pepper

■ If you can't find wild watercress in your area, domestic cress works just fine for this recipe. Blanch the watercress briefly in salted, boiling water to set the color. Then plunge or shock the cress in ice water to prevent overcooking. Shake the watercress dry and place it in a blender. Puree the watercress with the garlic, and slowly add the oil. Adjust seasonings at the end. Keep covered until needed, as the sauce will oxidize and turn brown if exposed for too long. Yields approximately two cups. Use the sauce to "paint" or accent your plates.

Kiln-Dried Cherry Chutney

1 pound kiln-dried cherries
¼ cup red wine vinegar
1½ cups pinot noir
2 tbsp brown sugar
⅛ tsp coriander seeds, ground
2 whole cloves, ground
¼ cup orange juice
1 tbsp orange zest
1 tbsp fresh ginger
1 tbsp garlic, minced
2 tsp thyme
1 tsp cinnamon
½ cup hazelnuts, toasted and
  chopped

■ Place the cherries and the wine in a small bowl. Allow this to seep for a few hours or overnight. Then heat a small sauce pan and cook the cherries over medium heat until they begin to soften. Add the vinegar, orange juice, zest, and the herbs and spices. Reduce until somewhat thick. Roast the hazelnuts on a sheet pan in a pre-heated 350° oven. Remove the skins by rubbing the hazelnuts in a clean towel while they are still hot. Rough chop them and add to the chutney mixture. Allow the chutney to cool or serve warm.

Braised Cattail Shoots*

16 cattail shoots, peeled to tender
  stocks
1 tbsp garlic, minced
1 lemon, juice of
1 tbsp fennel or caraway, crushed
2 tbsp olive oil
1 cup white stock
salt and pepper to taste

■ For this preparation, peel the shoots down to the most tender part, discarding the woody exterior. Pre-heat a straight-sided pan over medium heat. Add the oil, garlic, and cattails, and toss until the shoots are coated with the fat. Add the fennel, lemon juice, and white stock (see "Basic Recipes") and bring to a boil. Cover and cook until the cattails are tender, approximately 15 to 20 minutes. Season to taste.

Sautéed Fiddlehead Ferns with Morels

24 fiddleheads, cleaned
24 morel mushrooms
1 tomato, diced
1 tsp garlic, minced
4 tbsp whole butter
1 tbsp thyme, minced
1 tbsp parsley, minced
salt and pepper to taste

■ Fiddleheads, or fiddlenecks, are the new leaves or fronds of certain edible ferns found along the edges of streams and lakes. The most common is the pasture brake or Western bracken. When the new leaves first develop in spring, they are coiled like the upper part of a bass fiddle or violin, but they remain in this crunchy stage for only a few days. They are sweet and delicious.

■ For this preparation, pre-heat a sauté pan over high heat. Add the butter and melt, but do not burn. Add the cleaned fiddleheads and turn them frequently. Add the garlic and morel mushrooms, then the tomato and herbs. The tomato should break down and form a fondue, which will act as the sauce and add richness to the dish. Remove from heat and adjust the seasonings. Serve immediately.

Smoked Wild Turkey Cotelettes with Wild Boar Bacon, Wild Watercress Sauce, Kiln-Dried Cherry Chutney, Braised Cattail Shoots, Fiddlehead Ferns with Morels, Potato and Parsnip Cakes, and Onion Crispies (continued)

Yukon Gold and Parsnip Cakes

1 pound Yukon Gold potatoes, washed and peeled

1 Walla Walla sweet onion, peeled

2 parsnips, washed and peeled

1 tbsp garlic, minced

2 eggs

salt and pepper to taste

6 tbsp vegetable oil

Grate the potatoes, onion, and parsnips with a food processor or hand grater. If the onion produces a lot of liquid, strain it off through a cheesecloth (excessive onion milk will bitter the recipe). Add the garlic, salt, and pepper to the grated mixture. Beat the eggs slightly and mix them into the mixture. Pre-heat a non-stick sauté pan over medium heat. Add the oil and heat. Form small patties and pan-fry over medium heat until golden brown on each side. Drain on a paper towel and serve hot.

Onion Crispies

2 Walla Walla sweet onions, sliced very thin

2 cups flour

1 tbsp salt

1 tbsp black pepper

pinch thyme, parsley, paprika

2 cups vegetable oil

This is a great garnish for game dishes. The crisp onions add texture to a wide variety of plates, and they can also be eaten as a snack. To prepare, pre-heat the oil to 375 degrees in a tall sauce pan or use a deep fryer. Add the herbs and spices to the flour and toss the onions with the flour mixture. Avoid doing this too far in advance, because they stick together and become an ugly mess. Fry the onions in the pre-heated oil until crisp and brown. Drain on a paper towel and serve hot.

*Cattail, *Typha Latifolia*, is also known as Cossack asparagus, flags, or bulrushes, and grows in marshes and shallow ponds. Cattails grow from three to nine feet tall, and nearly all parts can be eaten at varying times of the year. In spring the new, tender shoots are eaten raw or briefly steamed or boiled. They are great in salads, or as a side dish for wild game and waterfowl. During the late fall and winter, the roots are a good source of starch, and may be cooked just like potatoes—boiled and mashed, pan-fried, or roasted.

Thai-Roasted Venison with Sesame Shrimp
served with Ginger Barley Pilaf, Glazed Shiitake Spring Roll, and Long Bean Sauté

Prepared by Gregory C. Werry, C.W.C., Sous Chef • The Westin Hotel • Seattle, Washington   *Serves Eight*

Thai-Roasted Venison with Sesame Shrimp

1 venison loin cut into 8 pieces, 3 ½ ounces each

1 pound shrimp, peeled and deveined

2 tbsp grated ginger

1½ tbsp garlic, minced

2 tsp lime zest

salt and pepper to taste

½ cup cream

2 tbsp cilantro

1 cup sesame seeds

▨ Season venison loin with olive oil, salt, and pepper. Sear quickly in a very hot pan, then remove from heat and cool. Prepare shrimp paste by combining shrimp, ginger, garlic, lime zest, salt, pepper, and cream, and pureeing until smooth. Spread two ounces of shrimp paste squarely on a piece of clear wrap. Place a cooled venison loin on top, and wrap so the outside of the loin is coated with shrimp paste. Open the clear wrap, and roll the loin in sesame seeds. Repeat process for all loin pieces. In a heavy sauté pan, sear the outside of the loins. Place in a 350° oven for about eight minutes, or until medium rare. Set aside.

Ginger Barley Pilaf

1 tbsp shallots, minced

1 tbsp ginger, grated

½ tbsp garlic, minced

3 tbsp olive oil

⅝ cup barley

3 cups chicken stock

1 bay leaf

salt and pepper to taste

3 tbsp chives, chopped

▨ Sauté shallots, ginger, and garlic in olive oil. Add barley, stirring to coat the barley. Add hot chicken stock until previous ingredients are covered by 1/2 inch. Bring to a simmer, cover, and cook until the barley is soft, plump, and dry (approximately 50 minutes). Fold in the chives and adjust seasonings.

Glazed Shiitake Spring Rolls

1 cup shiitake mushrooms, small diced

1 tsp garlic, minced

½ cup onion, small diced

½ cup carrot, small diced

½ cup cucumber, small diced

2 tsp cilantro, chopped

2 tsp fish sauce

2 tbsp corn starch slurry

salt and pepper to taste

▨ Sear shiitake in a heavy pan. Add garlic, onion, carrot, and cucumber. Cook out the flavors. Add cilantro and deglaze the pan with fish sauce. Reduce until dry. Bind the mixture with cornstarch slurry, and season to taste. Spread out to cool. Place approximately two tbsp of filling into a spring roll wrapper and wrap per instructions on package. Hold until ready to deep fry.

Thai-Roasted Venison with Sesame Shrimp, Ginger Barley Pilaf, Glazed Shiitake Spring Roll, and Long Bean Sauté (continued)

Lemon Grass Broth

1 quart chicken stock

2 inches ginger root

2 stalks lemon grass

1 tsp garlic

1 cup shiitake mushrooms, sliced

3 tbsp fish sauce

3 tbsp lime juice

1 tbsp roast chili paste

⅔ cup tomatoes, chopped

4 tbsp scallions

10 mint leaves

▇ Combine chicken stock, ginger root, lemon grass, and garlic. Simmer for 20 minutes, then strain to obtain broth. Sear the mushrooms. Add remaining ingredients. Deglaze the pan with broth. Use as a broth and sauce for the roasted venison. To create roast chili paste, peel and deseed peppers. Roast peppers, then puree into a paste.

To serve: Use a large, deep plate. Place the pilaf in a ring mold. Slice the spring roll on a bias, revealing the colors with your angle cut, and place it on plate. Slice venison loin and shingle the slices to the side of the pilaf. Garnish with long beans. Ladle on the broth, and garnish with cilantro leaves (optional).

Smoked and Seared Medallions of Wild Pheasant and Venison Loin

with Roasted Pepper Oil and Foie Gras Pudding, served with Fresh Mango Chutney

Prepared by Raul P. Lacara, Chef • Nob Hill Restaurant • San Francisco, California   *Serves Four*

Pheasant and Venison Loin

4 pheasant breasts
15-ounce venison loin
2 tbsp olive oil
1 bunch fresh thyme, chopped
dash salt and pepper

■ Season the pheasant and venison loin, then rub with olive oil and fresh thyme. Sear the venison loin and smoke the pheasant breast. Rest meat for ten minutes. Cut the venison loin into four pieces. Flatten pheasant breasts with meat hammer to tenderize, and stuff one portion of venison into each breast. Tie them with string and sear them slowly. When done, be sure the venison is medium rare (120° internal temperature). Slice gently into medallions.

To serve: Stand fried rice paper on plate and place chutney at base. Shingle the medallions on the plate. Remove foie gras pudding and add to plate near rice paper. Dot plate with red pepper oil or drizzle around dish.

Foie Gras Pudding

500 grams goose liver, Grade A
5 egg yolks
1 whole egg
¼ cup port wine
3 tbsp heavy cream
dash nutmeg
50 grams unsalted butter
pink salt (or sea salt) to taste

■ Clean the goose liver and set it out for about 30 minutes at room temperature. Combine all seasonings and all remaining ingredients except egg yolks and heavy cream. Place these in food processor and blend. Slowly add the egg yolks and heavy cream. When texture and taste are smooth, strain. Gently pour mixture in molding cups, first rubbing the cups evenly with unsalted butter. Place in waterbath and cook for about 20 minutes in a 300° oven.

Mango Chutney

2 ripe mangoes
2 red jalapeno peppers
2 green jalapeno peppers
½ red onion
½ cup Japanese rice wine vinegar
2 tbsp olive oil
4 slices rice paper
salt and pepper to taste

■ Peel and dice the mangoes, jalapeno peppers, and red onions. Mix remainder of ingredients and marinate chutney for two hours before serving.

Garnish

■ Slice red pepper in cold water and deep fry rice paper.

Roasted Red Pepper Oil

1 red bell pepper
¼ cup olive oil
dash cayenne pepper
salt and pepper to taste

■ Roast the red bell pepper over high heat until skin turns black. Peel and clean. Place in a blender with olive oil, dash of cayenne, and salt and pepper to taste.

Braised Stuffed Venison Shanks

with Pheasant Champagne Truffle Risotto, Red Lentils, and Spring Vegetables

Prepared by Michael Rork, Executive Chef • Harbor Court Hotel • Baltimore, Maryland　　　　　*Serves Six*

Braised Stuffed Venison Shanks with Pheasant

6 venison shanks

1½ pounds pheasant meat, thigh and breast

caul fat

3 sprigs fresh thyme

¼ cup chives

½ cup bacon

½ cup heavy cream

pinch fennel

2 eggs

3 shallots

3 cloves garlic

¼ cup brandy

5 bay leaves

¼ cup butter

¼ cup olive oil

1¼ cups mirepoix

2 quarts veal demi-glace

salt and pepper

1 cup red lentils

¼ cup corn starch

¼ cup cold water

■ Begin by removing all silver skin from shanks. Peel meat down to the knuckle (bone joint), sprinkle with salt and pepper, and refrigerate.

Separate thigh and breast meat from pheasant, dice, and marinate in brandy for three hours. Add shallots, garlic, thyme, and bacon. Place in a food processor and grind until smooth. Add eggs, heavy cream, chives, fennel, and salt and pepper. Place the forcemeat around the bone of the shank, wrap the meat of the shank around the forcemeat, then wrap each shank in caul fat, leaving bone exposed. Place in a braiser on high heat, adding butter and oil. Brown both sides, then remove to a 1/2" deep roasting pan. Pour the demi stock, mirepoix, and bay leaves over the shanks. Cover the pan with aluminum foil, pierce two holes in foil so steam can escape, and bake for one hour at 375°. After one hour, reduce oven to 325° and cook for an additional 90 minutes. Remove shanks from braising liquid and skim the fat. Place the stock in a pot, add lentils, and cook until tender. Thicken the sauce with corn starch and water, and adjust seasoning with salt and pepper.

Champagne Truffle Risotto

1 pound risotto

⅜ cup truffle peelings

⅜ cup parmesan cheese

2 cups chicken stock

½ cup olive oil

1 cup champagne

½ cup heavy cream

■ Place risotto and olive oil in a heavy-bottomed sauce pot, then stir over medium heat. Slowly add the chicken stock, a little at a time, until all stock is absorbed. Risotto should be sticky, but not fully cooked. Add champagne and truffles, and reduce. At serving time, add cream and parmesan cheese, reducing until everything comes together and risotto is tender.

To serve: Place risotto at one corner of plate and one shank next to the risotto. Place vegetables: one spring leek, three asparagus, and three julienned red peppers per plate. If you wish, use rosemary, tempura orange, and lemon rind in small mounds around the shank as garnish. Sauce the shank, place tempura orange and lemon rind atop the sauce, and serve.

Sautéed Stuffed Quail Breast

with Fennel, Brie, and Prosciutto in an Herb Crust with Truffle Merlot Sauce, Bacon and Thyme Stuffed Bliss Potatoes

Prepared by Jamie Boelhower, Chef • President's Room, Milwaukee Athletic Club • Milwaukee   *Serves Eight*

Sautéed Stuffed Quail Breast with Fennel, Brie, and Prosciutto

8 quail breasts, boneless
¾ pound prosciutto ham
one pound fennel, blanched
one pound brie cheese

▦ Trim excess fat from quail breasts. Stuff quail with blanched fennel, brie, and prosciutto ham. Fold breasts. Flour the breasts, dip in eggwash, and dredge in herb crust (below). Sauté and bake in oven to medium rare (120° internal temperature).

Herb Crust

1½ cups fresh bread crumbs
¼ cup fresh rosemary, chopped
¼ cup thyme, chopped
3 tbsp garlic, chopped
¼ cup gorgonzola cheese
flour and eggwash as needed

▦ Grate bread crumbs. Assemble the rosemary, thyme, garlic, and gorgonzola cheese, and chop finely. Mix all ingredients well.

Truffle Merlot Sauce

¾ cup whole truffles, sliced
1 shallot, minced
1 clove garlic, minced
¼ cup brown sugar
1 bottle merlot wine
1 quart quail stock (or chicken stock)
salt and pepper to taste
2 tsp arrowroot

▦ In a heated sauce pan, sweat shallot, truffles, and garlic. Deglaze with merlot wine and reduce by one-third. Add quail stock and reduce again by one-third. Add brown sugar and adjust seasonings. Thicken with arrowroot.

Bacon and Thyme Stuffed Bliss Potatoes

8 bliss potatoes
2 pounds bacon, chopped
¼ cup thyme
salt and pepper to taste
paprika to taste

▦ Cut two ends off each potato. Use a melon baller to hollow out one end of each. Brush with oil. Mix chopped bacon and thyme together. Fill hollowed ends with bacon and thyme, and sprinkle with excess thyme and paprika. Bake.

Braised Rabbit with Rabbit Chops and Roulade of Quail, Prosciutto, and Asiago

served with Cannellini Beans, Sautéed Spinach, and Chestnut Puree

Prepared by Benjamin Bailey, AM Sous Chef • Omni Hotel • Houston, Texas   *Serves Four*

Braised Rabbit

1 rabbit
½ cup pommace oil
2 large carrots
½ bunch of celery
3 large onions
1 cup mixed mushrooms
1 bottle cabernet sauvignon
strong brown chicken stock, enough
   to cover
salt and pepper
2 bay leaves
¼ cup tomato paste
¼ cup brandy

■ When butchering rabbit, remove legs. Detach loin end of rabbit just below the last rib. Split the rack, remove the chin bone, and French cut the rib bones. Butcher can prepare the rabbit for you. Wrap both racks in caul fat (optional), with the bones exposed. Dice the loin, leg, and thigh meat. Season, then sear in smoking pommace oil. When thoroughly browned, remove from pan. Add the diced onions and mushrooms and brown them. Add diced carrots and celery and sweat these ingredients. Pince (see glossary) with tomato paste. Wrap the rabbit pieces in a cheese cloth. Return rabbit to pan. Deglaze with red wine, and reduce until thickened. Add enough stock to almost cover the rabbit. Bring to a boil, cover the pan, and place in 300° oven for 2-1/2 hours. When easily penetrated with a fork, remove the rabbit sachet and strain sauce. Reduce the sauce to desired consistency and flavor, adding the brandy before reducing. Finish the sauce by whipping in butter and a little lemon juice.

Quail Roulade

4 quails
4 thin slices prosciutto
4 shaved pieces asiago
chopped herbs

■ Remove legs and wings from the quail and set aside. Pound breast meat lightly, skin-side down, with a meat hammer until a thin square. Season with salt, pepper, and herbs. Lay down prosciutto, then asiago. Roll and tie. Season, then brown in sauté pan. Finish in a 375° oven to medium doneness (approximately five minutes).

Cannellini Beans

1 cup onion, diced
½ cup carrot, diced
½ cup celery, diced
1 cup cannellini beans, soaked
½ cup sun-dried tomatoes, soaked
   and julienned
1 bay leaf
salt and pepper to season
olive oil
2½ cups strong chicken stock
1 cup white wine

■ Heat onions in olive oil until translucent. Add carrots and celery, and sweat. Add sun-dried tomatoes, and sweat. Add white wine and reduce. Add beans, then add stock, bay leaf, and seasoning. Cook until tender, adding more stock if necessary.

Chestnut Puree

1 cup chestnuts, blanched
¼ cup heavy cream
½ tsp nutmeg
1 tsp brown sugar
salt and pepper

■ Simmer chestnuts in cream. Add nutmeg and brown sugar. Salt and pepper to taste, and puree in food processor.

Rabbit Chops

■ Season and brown the racks of ribs by searing in a hot skillet or sauté pan. Finish in a 325° oven to 145° internal temperature. Create chops by cutting between each bone.

Antelope Ragout
with Goose Prosciutto, Smoked Duck Sausage, and Potato Galette

Prepared by Bill Morris, C.W.C. • Chef de Cuisine, Rover's Restaurant • Seattle, Washington

---

Ragout

½ cup butter

1 pound antelope shoulder

4 tbsp carrots, diced small

4 tbsp onion, diced small

3 tbsp celery, diced small

4 tbsp shallots

3 tbsp garlic, diced small

2 tbsp thyme

2 tbsp oregano

2 tbsp black peppercorns, crushed

2 bay leaves

6 shiitake mushrooms

½ cup tomato, chopped

½ cup balsamic vinegar

¾ cup red wine

6 cups game stock

¾ cup red currant jelly

½ cup goose prosciutto

Heat whole butter and sear antelope completely at high heat. Remove from pan and add mirepoix (vegetables). Sauté until caramelized, then add herbs, spices, mushrooms, and tomato. Deglaze pan with vinegar and reduce to jelly-like glaze. Add wine and reduce by half. Add hot stock, simmer, then return meat to stock. Cook covered in the oven at medium temperature until tender (approximately one hour). Remove meat and reduce sauce until syrupy. Add the jelly, prosciutto, and remaining butter, and season.

Potato Galette

4 potatoes

2 eggs

2 tbsp parsley

Peel potatoes and shred fine. Add eggs, parsley, and seasoning and mix ingredients well. Press into ring molds and transfer into a hot sauté pan. Brown on both sides, and finish in oven.

Duck Sausage

½ pound duck meat

4 sprigs rosemary

¼ cup pistachios

2 tbsp parsley

¼ tsp allspice

¼ tsp clove

¼ tsp mace

about one foot of casing

Small dice the duck meat and marinate in rosemary and spices. Grind through a sausage machine, using first a large die, then a medium die. Finely chop the pistachios and parsley, and add these to the duck. Put in a mixer with a paddle attachment, and mix until well emulsified. Season, then pipe into the casing. (Sausage can also be obtained directly from butcher.) Smoke, poach, and grill.

Lentil Timbale

½ cup French green lentils

1 tbsp shallots

½ tbsp garlic

1 tbsp thyme

2 tbsp tarragon

¼ pound bacon

4 eggs

½ cup cream

1 tbsp parsley

1 cup apple cider

½ cup chicken stock

Sweat shallots and garlic with the lentils, then add apple cider. Reduce by half, add chicken stock, and bring to boil. Cook until tender. Mince bacon and render in hot pan, removing fat. Chop herbs fine. Mix cooled lentils, bacon, and herbs with eggs and cream. Season, then portion into timbale molds. Cook covered in a water bath at 300° for about one hour, then remove from molds.

Pan-Seared Peppered Pheasant Breast
with Dried Cherry, Balsamic Vinegar, and Port Wine Sauce

Prepared by Ronald Bohnert, Executive Chef • Radisson Hotel St. Paul • St. Paul, Minnesota   *Serves Four*

Pan-Seared Peppered Pheasant Breast

4 boned pheasant breasts, skin-on, wing joint attached

3 tbsp five-peppercorn blend, coarse ground

¼ tsp salt

▨ Rinse pheasant and tap dry. Rub with peppercorn mixture and salt. In a hot, heavy-bottomed pan, sear pheasant breasts on skin side first; then turn over and sear bottom. Place pheasant on a heated plate in 350° oven until medium rare (120° internal temperature). Remove from oven and keep warm. Reserve leg and thighs for making smoked pheasant meat for another occasion. Reserve carcass for pheasant demi-glace.

Dried Cherry, Balsamic Vinegar, and Port Wine Sauce

1 cup dried cherries

⅓ cup Roland balsamic vinegar

2 cups Sandeman port wine

1½ cups pheasant demi-glace (or chicken stock)

2 tbsp unsalted butter, chilled

▨ Simmer cherries in port wine. When cherries are plump, set 1/4 cup aside for garnish. Add balsamic vinegar and simmer two to three minutes. Remove from heat and add to pheasant demi-glace. Puree with food processor and return to stove. Bring to simmer and skim. Fold in chilled butter.

To serve: Place sauce on bottom of plate. Slice pheasant breast into five slices and fan out on top of sauce. Garnish with enoki mushrooms, fresh thyme sprig, croquette potatoes shaped like mushrooms, and the dried cherries set aside earlier.

Cardamom-Cured Venison Steaks

with Venison Confit Tamale, Black Bean Salsa, and Cranberry Ancho Chutney

Prepared by Mark Haugen, Executive Chef • Tejas Restaurant • Minneapolis, Minnesota   *Serves Eight*

Venison Confit

2-pound venison shoulder, round or loin

1 cup yellow onion, julienned

½ tsp thyme, finely chopped

½ tsp rosemary, finely chopped

½ tsp sage, finely chopped

½ tsp basil, finely chopped

½ tsp cilantro, finely chopped

6 cloves fresh garlic, finely chopped

1 tsp salt

1 tsp black pepper, ground

½ gallon beef stock

■ Preheat oven to 300°. Trim all fat and silver skin from venison. Mix the herbs, salt, garlic, and pepper. Rub the meat with the mixture. Sear the venison with onion in a hot skillet (large) or roasting pan until well browned. Add beef stock and bring to a simmer. Cover pan and place in oven for two hours. Remove and allow venison to cool thoroughly in beef stock. Shred venison. Reduce beef stock to 1/2 cup on stovetop and mix it with the shredded venison.

Tamales

1½ cups fresh corn kernels

⅝ cup vegetable shortening

½ cup masa harina (or all-purpose flour)

¾ cup yellow cornmeal

1 tsp salt

½ tsp cayenne pepper

½ tsp cumin

■ Place shortening in mixing bowl and whip until soft. Add masa harina, cornmeal, salt, cayenne pepper, and cumin. Set aside. Bring four cups of salted water to a boil. Add corn kernels and cook for three minutes. Drain corn and grind it in a food processor until smooth. Remove from processor and add to the cornmeal mixture, mixing until a semi-sticky consistency is achieved. Set aside. Makes eight tamales.

■ To assemble each venison tamale, spread about 3/8 cup of the corn masa onto a 5" by 5" piece of plastic wrap. Be sure to leave enough room at the end of the plastic wrap to roll and tie the tamale. Add three ounces of the venison confit into the center of the corn masa. Roll the plastic and tie each end. Steam tamales for 20 minutes.

Black Bean Salsa

1 cup onions, ¼" dice

½ cup carrots, ¼" dice

2 ribs celery, ¼" dice

6 cups black beans, sorted for stones and rinsed

1 quart chicken or veal stock (or canned chicken broth)

2 tbsp cilantro, finely chopped

1 cup dry white wine

8 ounces fresh orange juice

4 cloves garlic, minced

3 tbsp epazote, finely chopped

1 tbsp ground cumin

2 tsp chili powder

1 tbsp salt

1 tsp white pepper

1 tbsp vegetable shortening

1 orange, zest of, blanched in two cups boiling water for three minutes

4 jalapeno peppers, seeded and minced

■ Heat shortening in a heavy, one-gallon sauce pot. Add onion and cook until well browned. Stir in all remaining ingredients except the epazote and cilantro. Bring to a boil and simmer until beans are very soft and begin to break apart. Then stir in epazote and cilantro, and keep warm (or reheat later). Makes 1-1/2 quarts.

Cranberry Ancho Chutney

4 cups cranberries

4 ancho chiles

1 red bell pepper, peeled, seeded, and ¼" diced

1 green bell pepper, peeled, seeded, and ¼" diced

1 yellow bell pepper, peeled, seeded, and ¼" diced

1 small red onion, ¼" diced

1 cup white wine vinegar

1 cup sugar

1 bay leaf

1 tsp ground cumin

½ tsp ground coriander

1 tsp ground allspice

½ tsp ground black pepper

1 tsp salt

1 tbsp cilantro, chopped fine

1 tbsp basil

▪ To prepare the ancho chiles, cover them with warm water and roast in a 350° oven for two minutes, or until soft. Then julienne the soft ancho chilies. Bring all ingredients except basil and cilantro to a boil in a heavy sauce pan. Reduce heat to a simmer and cook until cranberries break apart and chutney is thick. Stir in basil and cilantro and set aside. Makes two cups. Serve warm with tamales.

Cardamom-Cured Venison Steaks

24 2-ounce venison steaks

¾ cup cardamom, ground

¼ cup salt

4 tbsp black pepper, ground

1 cup cabernet sauvignon

½ cup corn oil

½ cup clarified butter

▪ Trim all fat and silver skin from venison. Mix all ingredients except butter, and marinate venison for up to four hours. Heat a skillet with clarified butter and sear venison steaks for three minutes on each side.

To serve: Ladle three ounces of salsa on each plate. Place one tamale in center of each plate. Surround tamale with three venison steaks. Spoon one tablespoon of chutney between each venison steak and serve.

The Outback Platter

Prepared by William Aschenbrenner, C.E.C./A.A.C.,
Executive Chef • The Mar-a-Lago Club • Palm Beach, Florida

Serves Four

Braised Loin of Black Bear Wrapped in Savory Cabbage

4 3-ounce center cut black bear tenderloins
1 head savory cabbage

■ Season the bear tenderloins and grill or broil them until medium rare (110° internal temperature). Clean and blanch the savory cabbage, then wrap tenderloins in cabbage.

Wild Berry Au Jus

½ pint wild black or red raspberries (or store-bought)
1 cup lamb or beef stock

■ Clean the berries, puree, and cook until reduced to stock. Add the meat stock and heat through.

Alligator, Black Bean, and Tomato Ravioli Filling

½ pound alligator tail
⅓ cup black beans, soaked
1 tomato, field ripe

■ Grind the alligator tail, sauté, and cool. To prepare the black beans, soak them in cold water for at least four hours (or overnight) to expedite the cooking process. Rinse beans well and place them in a sauce pan. Cover with water (one quart per cup of beans),

add one tbsp of baking soda, and bring to a boil. Reduce heat to a simmer, skim the top, and cook until beans are tender. When beans are cool, mix them with the alligator. Poach the tomato, then peel, deseed, and mix with the beans.

Roast Red Bell Pepper Sauce

3 red bell peppers
¼ cup heavy cream

■ Roast the red bell peppers, peel, and puree. Fold cream into the peppers.

Field Vegetable Brunoise

1 large carrot
1 medium zucchini
16 asparagus
salt
ground black pepper
fresh mint
thyme
rosemary

■ Clean carrot and zucchini, then peel and dice a la Brunoise (small-dice). Clean asparagus, poach, and season all vegetables.

Ravioli Pasta

6 tbsp butter
1 egg
⅓ cup flour
⅛ cup milk

■ Mix butter, egg, flour, and milk together for ravioli. Stuff pasta and place in salted, boiling water until ravioli rides to the top. Let cook for one minute longer and remove from water.

Venison and Herb Sausage

5 ounces venison
fresh herbs
casing (for sausage)

■ Seasoning and herbs for sausage include salt, ground black pepper, fresh mint, thyme, and rosemary. Grind the venison, season with fresh herbs, and stuff in sausage casing. Poach sausage in boiling water until done.

Filet of Venison, Woodlands Style

Prepared by Jerry Peters, C.E.C./A.A.C., Executive Chef • Enchantment Resort • Sedona, Arizona   *Serves Four*

Smoked Chile Demi-glace

1 quart venison or veal stock
1 cup apple cider
¼ cup dried wild mushrooms
6 fresh sage leaves, chopped
2 bay leaves
1 tbsp fresh thyme
1 tsp juniper berries, crushed
1 tbsp cracked black pepper
4 garlic cloves, crushed
5 dried chipotles (smoked jalapenos)
8 to 10 prickly pears, peeled
1 cup prickly pear juice
2 tbsp rice vinegar

■ Place the stock, apple cider, mushrooms, herbs, spices, garlic, chiles, and pepper in a heavy sauce pot. Gradually reduce by half over low heat, skimming often. Add whole prickly pears (or pomegranate if not available) and continue to reduce slowly, breaking up fruits until mixture becomes syrupy and lightly coats the back of a wooden spoon. Puree sauce in a blender, then pass through a fine sieve. Stir in rice vinegar and prickly pear juice. (Pomegranate or apple juice may be substituted.)

Mushroom Duxelle

1 cup mushrooms
¼ cup shiitake mushrooms
⅓ cup pine nuts, roasted
1 Anaheim chile pepper
2 tsp red jalapeno, diced
1 tbsp shallot, chopped
2 garlic cloves, crushed
¼ cup Madeira wine
¼ cup heavy cream
salt and pepper to taste

■ Fine chop the first seven ingredients in a food processor. Place in a heavy sauce pan with the wine, heavy cream, and salt and pepper. Cook on low heat, stirring until all liquid evaporates. Cool.

Filets

4 6-ounce venison filets
2 potatoes
½ cup butter
salt and pepper to taste

■ Cut a small pocket in the side of each filet. Slice the potatoes lengthwise and paper-thin with a grater or food processor and set aside. Season the filets with salt and pepper and sear them in a large, hot skillet. Set aside. When filets are still slightly warm, spoon some of the mushroom duxelle into the pockets, then press together to seal well. Take the thin slices of potato and wrap them around each filet, pressing gently so the potatoes adhere to the filets. Repeat the process a second time. Melt butter in a heavy skillet, being careful not to let the butter brown. Sauté the filets until the potatoes are nicely browned and crisp. Turn the filets over for just a minute to finish cooking the meat, then blot off the excess oil on paper towel.

To serve: Cover plate with some of the smoked chile demi-glace and place filet on top.

The Rest of the Best

Selected Recipes from the Original National
Wild Game Cooking Competition

Alligator Tacos with Sweet Ancho Chile Sauce
served with Chorizo Sausage Arroz and Black Bean Salsa

Submitted by Stanley F. Tom–The Union House–Genesee Depot, Wisconsin   *Serves Four*

Taco Shells

1½ cup flour
½ cup milk
1 egg
1 tsp cumin, ground
salt and pepper to taste

■ Mix all the ingredients together. In a sauté pan make thin, six-inch pancakes or crepes with batter. Remove from pan and set aside.

Taco Filling

½ pound alligator meat, cubed
1 cup fresh spinach, chopped
1 cup Monterey Jack cheese, shredded
½ cup onions, diced

■ Sauté alligator with two tablespoons of ancho chile sauce. Add all ingredients to taco shell, then spoon ancho chile sauce over tacos. Add a few shreds of cheese. Preheat oven at broil setting and bake in oven until cheese is melted.

Sweet Ancho Chile Sauce

¼ cup ancho chiles, pureed
6 cups water
½ onion, diced
1 tomato, deseeded and diced
4 jalapenos, deseeded and diced
2 cups brown sauce
2 tbsp Marsala wine
½ cup maple syrup
4 tbsp whipping cream
cornstarch or arrowroot for
    thickening

■ Add the pureed chiles, diced onion, tomato, and jalapenos to water. Cook and reduce for 30 minutes. Add brown sauce and wine, then reduce another 15 minutes. Add maple syrup, then reduce 15 minutes. If needed, thicken slightly with cornstarch or arrowroot, then add whipping cream. Reduce 10 to 15 minutes more, then remove from heat and let sit.

Chorizo Sausage Arroz

1 cup white rice
2 cups water
½ cup corn kernels
½ cup red bell pepper, diced
¾ cup chorizo sausage

■ Bring rice and water to boil, then simmer uncovered for 20 minutes. Add other ingredients and cover. Simmer for 30 minutes. Remove from heat and set aside for use in taco.

Black Bean Salsa

2 cups black beans, cooked
1 cup tomato, deseeded and diced
½ cup shallots, chopped
1 tbsp garlic, chopped
2 tbsp fresh cilantro, chopped
1 jalapeno pepper, deseeded and
    diced
½ cup lime juice
salt and pepper to taste

■ Mix all ingredients together. Let stand in cooler for one hour. Set aside for use in taco.

For Simplicity's Sake:

A casual creation demonstrating how well alligator lends itself to the well-known Mexican specialty, tacos. You can buy the taco shells at a grocery store, but making them is part of the fun. Rehydrate the chiles (soak them in water) before using them.

To serve: Put tacos on plate and add filling. Complement with sausage arroz and black bean salsa.

Antelope Chop with Ancho Raspberry Port Sauce
served with Tumbleweed Potatoes

Submitted by Andy Brooks • San Ysidro Ranch • Montecito, California

Serves Four

Antelope Chops and Pea Tendrils

8 antelope chops, 6 to 8 ounces, cleaned and trimmed

2 tsp cajun spice

½ cup fresh corn niblets

¼ cup tomato concasse

1 tbsp shallots, sliced

2 tbsp butter

1 cup pea tendrils

salt and pepper to taste

1 cup parsley, chopped

1 tbsp crushed red pepper

■ Season chops with cajun spice and grill to desired temperature. Set chops aside and keep them warm. Heat a sauté pan and add butter. When the butter is hot, add shallots, tomato concasse, and corn niblets. Sauté for two minutes, then remove from the heat. Add pea tendrils and salt and pepper, and toss quickly. Mix chopped parsley and red chili together and set aside.

Raspberry Port Sauce

1 cup port wine

⅓ cup raspberry jam

¼ cup ancho puree

½ cup veal or game glacé

1 tsp garlic, minced

1 tsp shallots, minced

■ Place port wine, garlic, and shallots in a sauce pan and reduce by half. Then whip in raspberry jam and ancho puree and bring to boil. Add veal stock, and cook until the sauce thickens. Strain and keep warm.

To serve: Place the pea tendril mix in the center of a plate, and arrange the tumbleweed potatoes around the mix. Criss-cross the chops in the center of the plate, and drizzle sauce around the outside of the plate.

Tumbleweed Potatoes

1 baking potato, peeled and grated

2 green onions, chopped

¼ yellow onion, finely chopped

½ egg, beaten

½ tsp baking powder

¼ cup all-purpose flour

¼ tsp ground cumin

salt and pepper to taste

1 cup olive oil

■ To make dough, mix the potato, green onions, yellow onion, and egg in a bowl. Sift baking powder and flour together, add to the potato mixture, season, then mix well. Heat one cup of oil in a skillet. Squeeze the dough through your fingers into the pan. Be careful not to let grease splatter onto your hand. Cook until golden brown.

For Simplicity's Sake:

Refer to "Basic Recipes" for a basic glacé recipe. You might substitute diced tomato for the concasse, and you can broil the chops in your oven instead of grilling them. Ancho puree is available wherever Mexican or Southwestern foods are sold. To make your own, use dried ancho peppers. Soak them in warm, salted water. When the pepper is soft, split it down the middle and scoop the pulp out with a spoon. You now have ancho puree. One caution: The puree can cause a painful burn to eyes and other sensitive areas. You'll love the tumbleweed potatoes.

Seared South Texas Antelope Eye of Round with Huckleberry Sauce

Submitted by Dakota • Pinon Grill • Hilton of Santa Fe • Santa Fe, New Mexico   *Serves Four*

Antelope Eye of Round

1 1½- to 2-pound eye of round, antelope

■ Rub eye of round with pepper rub (see below). Sear all sides of the antelope in a hot skillet, then transfer to a 425° oven. Roast about 15 minutes to an internal temperature of 110°. Remove from oven and let rest for about 15 minutes. Slice very thin.

Pepper Rub

5 tbsp black pepper, cracked
2 tbsp salt
1 tsp cayenne
4 tbsp lemon zest
3 tbsp fresh rosemary, chopped fine
3 tbsp fresh thyme, chopped fine
■ Mix all ingredients well.

Huckleberry Sauce

10 cups game stock
3 cloves garlic
3 clove
½ cinnamon stick
5 bay leaves
2 tbsp tomato paste
1 pound huckleberries, fresh or frozen
2 ounces rose water
1 tsp salt
■ Combine stock, garlic, cinnamon, bay leaves, and tomato paste in a sauce pan. Simmer over low heat, skimming the excess fat every ten minutes or so. Reduce to approximately three cups. Strain and discard herbs, reserving the liquid. Add liquid to sauce pan and bring to boil. Add huckleberries and simmer for 20 minutes. Add salt and pepper to taste. Just before serving, stir in the rose water.

To serve: Pour sauce over antelope.

For Simplicity's Sake:

This recipe makes fine use of a roast. Use fresh lemon zest by grating the rind from the lemon or using a potato peeler and chopping it finely. Rose water can be found in specialty or health stores. If you have huckleberries, use them, but if not you might substitute lingonberries or wild blueberries. For game stock or brown sauce, see "Basic Recipes."

Thai Hellfire Black Buck Antelope with Wild Rice Salad

Submitted by R. Hamilton Kabakoff, C.W.C. • Scottsdale Plaza Resort • Scottsdale, Arizona   *Serves Four*

Thai Hellfire Marinade

4 ounces cashews, roasted

½ cup red curry paste

¼ cup coconut milk

½ cup scallions, chopped

1 serrano pepper

1 tbsp honey

1 tbsp sesame oil

1 tbsp brown rice vinegar

1 tbsp cumin

½ tsp black pepper

½ tsp salt

■ Combine all ingredients in a food processor and blend until smooth.

To serve: Complement antelope slices with warm wild rice salad.

Antelope Loin

1½ pound antelope loin, cleaned and trimmed

■ Marinate antelope loin in marinade for at least one hour. Pre-heat oven to 450°. Remove loin from marinade and place on sheet pan. Roast in the oven for seven minutes, then lower the temperature to 325° and roast for five more minutes, or until antelope reaches 120° internal temperature (longer if desired). Allow antelope to rest for 15 minutes before slicing to serve.

Warm Wild Rice Salad with Smoked Portabello Mushrooms and Spinach

2 ounces olive oil

4 ounces wild rice, cooked

3 smoked portabello mushrooms, sliced

1 clove garlic, minced

½ tsp black pepper

¼ tsp kosher salt

½ cup fresh spinach, cleaned and julienned

fresh nutmeg to taste

⅛ tsp truffle oil

■ In a hot sauté pan, add olive oil. When the oil is hot, begin to sauté wild rice, mushrooms, and garlic. Season with salt and pepper. When rice is warm, add spinach and nutmeg. Finish with truffle oil.

For Simplicity's Sake:

Not for the meek of palate. Coconut milk is an excellent tenderizer in this marinade, and it can be found in most supermarkets. Avoid overuse of the sesame oil, which has a very strong flavor. You can substitute if brown rice vinegar is not available, but check with grocery stores and Oriental markets. Truffle oil, sometimes called "liquid gold," has become more popular, but use it in moderation. Look for it in specialty stores. If a grill is not accessible, you may roast the portabello mushroom, which is found in most supermarkets. To cook wild rice, see "Basic Recipes."

Bear Loin and Potato Lasagna with Carrot-Caraway Sauce

Submitted by Nicholas Petti • Cafe Trio • Chapel Hill, North Carolina　　　　　*Serves Four*

4 eight-ounce pieces bear loin,
   cleaned and trimmed
1 pound carrots, peeled and chopped
4 tbsp caraway seed, toasted
1 medium onion, chopped fine
2 celery stalks, chopped fine
1 qt chicken stock
1 bunch leeks, cleaned and sliced ¼"
   thick
2 russet potatoes, peeled and sliced
   thin, lengthwise
salt and pepper to taste
1 tbsp olive oil
4 tbsp butter, melted

■ In a sauce pan, sweat the carrots, onion, celery and three tablespoons of the caraway seeds. Add the chicken stock and cook until the carrots are very tender. Puree in a food processor, strain, and save the sauce.

■ Sauté the leeks with remaining caraway seed in olive oil until translucent and tender. Season with salt and pepper and set aside.

■ Season the bear with salt and pepper. Sear the bear on all sides in a very hot pan, then finish cooking in a 375° oven until medium rare. Remove from the oven and let meat rest.

■ Coat the potato slices with melted butter and lay on cookie sheet in a 200° oven for about five minutes. The potatoes should be al dente (firm in the center).

To serve: Pour sauce to cover the plate. Layer the potato slices, followed by a bed of leeks, then the bear slices. Top with potato slices to form the lasagna. If you wish, arrange steamed vegetables around border of the plate to garnish.

For Simplicity's Sake:

Here's a "potato pasta" lasagna with a great sauce. If you like, you can replace the leeks with sweet onions or a vegetable of your choice. Check "Basic Recipes" for a chicken stock recipe.

Braised Leg of Black Bear with Huckleberry and Caramelized Honey Sauce

Submitted by Milos Cihelka, C.M.C. • *The Golden Mushroom Restaurant* • *Southfield, Michigan*   *Serves Six*

Bear

6 pounds bear meat (hind leg),
    trimmed and cubed
¼ cup bacon fat
salt
1 cup port wine
2 cups rich brown stock

Marinade

1 tbsp garlic, minced
¼ cup lemon juice
½ cup olive oil
8 bay leaves
pinch of thyme
20 juniper berries, crushed
10 allspice berries, crushed
2 tbsp black peppercorns, crushed
1 celery stalk, sliced
1 carrot, peeled and sliced
½ medium onion, sliced

Sauce

½ cup honey
1 tbsp currant jelly
¼ ounce dark rum
¼ cup port wine
¾ cup huckleberries
2 tsp Chinese Five-Spice
¾ cup soft butter

■ Ask your butcher to tie the roasts from the hind leg. Combine all the marinade ingredients, mix well, and put the meat and marinade in a Tupperware container. Seal tightly and refrigerate. Marinate for three days, turning the meat daily.

■ To cook, clean the marinade off the meat. Preheat a skillet with bacon fat. Season the meat with salt and brown on all sides. Transfer the meat to a roasting pan. Now add the marinade vegetables to the skillet and brown them slightly. Add one cup of port wine, 1/4 cup of huckleberries, and the brown stock. Pour everything over the meat in the roasting pan. Cover and roast in a 300° oven, turning occasionally until tender (3 to 4 hours).

■ To make the sauce, transfer the meat to another dish, cover, and keep warm. Strain the remaining juices into a sauce pan. Meanwhile, place the honey in a suitable dish and bake in the same oven until it assumes a rich brown color. In the saucepan, rapidly reduce the juices with remaining port wine, dark rum, and currant jelly to desired taste and consistency. In a pan, sauté the huckleberries with Five-Spice and butter until warm. Add the huckleberries and caramelized honey to the sauce and simmer for five minutes.

To serve: Slice and top with sauce. Don't forget to remove the string!

For Simplicity's Sake:

If you take the time to follow this recipe, your reward will be twofold: the bear and the sauce. It's a wonderful combination of simple flavors. Juniper (and all spice berries) can be dried. You'll find Chinese 5-Spice at a supermarket or Oriental grocery store, or you can make your own (see glossary). Not a difficult recipe, and you can substitute canned or frozen huckleberries or use blueberries or lingonberries.

Sautéed Black Bear Cutlets
with Sun-Dried Fruit Confit

Submitted by George Habecker • Topton Hotel • Topton, Pennsylvania

Serves Four

Fruit Confit

½ cup blueberries, dried

½ cup cranberries, dried

½ cup cherries, dried

¾ cup white wine

½ tsp shallots, finely chopped

¼ cup honey

¼ cup balsamic vinegar

■ Combine fruits, wines, and shallots in a sauce pan. Simmer for 6 to 8 minutes, until most of the liquid is absorbed and the fruit is soft. Add honey and vinegar. Stir and remove from heat. Set aside.

Bear Cutlets

12 2-ounce black bear leg cutlets, cut across grain

4 ounces dry sherry

1 tbsp melted butter

½ tbsp demi-glace (or brown sauce)

½ tsp dijon mustard, whole grain

½ tsp prepared horseradish

flour to coat meat

salt and pepper to taste

■ Pound cutlets with meat hammer to 1/4" thickness. Flour the cutlets lightly. Heat butter in sauté pan, and sauté cutlets for approximately 1-1/2 minutes, until browned on both sides. Leaving cutlets in the pan, season with salt and pepper. Deglaze the pan with half the sherry. Reduce until pan is dry. Add mustard, demi-glace (brown sauce), horseradish, and remaining sherry. Stir until the sauce is smooth.

To serve: Place cutlets on the plate with sauce, and garnish with fruit confit.

For Simplicity's Sake:

You can't go wrong when you combine these three berries—dried, fresh, or frozen, they make a fine confit. Legends insist that bear meat is strong and gamey, but the bear's natural diet dictates that the meat is generally quite succulent. In terms of fat content, bear meat is similar to pork, and you can treat it like pork when cooking. There's no need to lard or baste it. Roasted, smoked ham has long been considered a delicacy.

Smoked Pepper-Crusted Saddle of Wild Boar with Sun-Dried Cherry/Port Sauce

Submitted by Gloria Ciccarone-Nehls • The Big Four Restaurant, Huntington Hotel • San Francisco   *Serves Six*

Wild Boar

3 quarts brine

1 3- to 4-pound loin of wild boar,
    partially trimmed with thin layer
    of fat

3 tbsp black and white peppercorns,
    crushed

3 tbsp dark rum

3 tbsp brown sugar

▪ Place boar in a container and cover completely with cooled brine. Marinate overnight or for 24 hours.

▪ Drain boar and rinse well under cold water, then pat dry. Coat meat on all sides with dried peppercorns. Sprinkle with dark rum, then spread a light coating of brown sugar over entire surface. Let sit under refrigeration for one hour.

▪ The boar is now ready to be smoked and roasted or simply cooked on your outdoor grill (a grill with a cover is preferable). Cook to medium doneness or until very slightly pink in the center. The internal temperature should be 150°, which may take about one hour depending on the temperature of your grill.

Brine

3 quarts water

½ cup salt

1½ cups brown sugar

1 lemon, zest of

1 orange, zest of

½ tsp peppercorns

1 bay leaf

2 cloves garlic, crushed

2 sprigs fresh thyme (or ¼ tsp dried)

▪ Combine all ingredients and bring to boil. Cool before using.

Sun-Dried Cherry/Port Sauce

2 tbsp butter, melted

5 shallots, finely diced

½ stalk celery, finely diced

½ yellow onion, finely diced

3 sprigs fresh thyme

½ tsp cracked black peppercorns

2 cups ruby port wine

2 cups brandy

4 ounces sun-dried cherries

8 cups very reduced veal stock or
    demi-glace

▪ Soak 1/2 cup of cherries in 1/2 cup of brandy, then set aside.

▪ Sauté the first six ingredients together in butter until lightly browned. Add port, remainder of brandy, and half of the soaking cherries to the mixture. Reduce until the mixture has the consistency of syrup. Add the eight cups of demi-glace (or stock). Bring to a boil and simmer for 15 minutes or until desired thickness is obtained. Skim the sauce and strain.

▪ Place remaining brandy and cherries in a heavy pan. Using a long-stemmed match, ignite the brandy and cherries to burn off the alcohol. When the flame has died out, add to the strained sauce as garnish.

To serve: Slice boar loin, plate, and serve with 1/4 cup of sauce per meat serving.

For Simplicity's Sake:

This recipe is bursting with complementary flavors. Please use caution while flaming your brandy and cherries. Chicken stock or game stock can be substituted for the veal stock (see "Basic Recipes").

Peppered Grilled Wild Boar Loin Chop with Chokecherry Sauce

Submitted by Timothy "Red" Grenell • University Club • St. Paul, Minnesota

Serves Four

Wild Boar Loin Chops

4 12-ounce wild boar loin chops,
   cleaned & trimmed
5 sprigs rosemary
4 ounces black pepper, cracked
4 cloves garlic, diced
¼ cup olive oil

■ Pound garlic and pepper into wild boar chops, then marinate in olive oil.

■ Remove chops from marinade and pat dry. Grill or broil in oven, cooking until medium rare (120° internal temperature).

Chokecherry Sauce

¾ cup chokecherries
2 cups wild boar stock or brown
   sauce
4 tbsp shallots, minced
2 tbsp garlic, minced
¼ cup port wine
2 tbsp balsamic vinegar
2 tbsp sugar
24 rosemary leaves
4 ounces cold butter
salt and pepper to taste

■ Sauté the chokecherries, shallots, and garlic for two minutes. Add port wine, vinegar, sugar, and half of the rosemary leaves. Reduce to one-half and caramelize. Add boar stock or brown sauce and reduce again by one-half. Season with salt and pepper. Whip the butter in last.

To serve: Place sauce over chops and garnish with rosemary.

For Simplicity's Sake:

At one time, cherries were commonly and naturally used with most wild game meats. This straightforward dish is a winner on the grill or in the oven. For game stock or brown sauce, see "Basic Recipes."

Roast Wild Boar Chop
with Red Curry and Lemon Grass Crust

Submitted by Rick Valenzuela • Woodlands Plaza Hotel • Flagstaff, Arizona   *Serves Two*

Wild Boar Chop

2 7-ounce wild boar chops, cleaned
   and trimmed

3 ounces red curry and lemon grass
   paste

■ Season the boar chops with salt,
and spread the paste (see right) over
each side of the chops.

■ In a hot sauté pan, brown both
sides. Finish in a 500° oven. Cook
until medium rare (internal
temperature of 120°).

To serve: Pour boar jus on the plate.
Place the chop on the jus. Serve with
grilled vegetables and noodles.

Red Curry and Lemon Grass Paste

15 red chili peppers, deseeded and
   diced

2 stalks lemon grass, coarsely
   chopped

5 shallots, thinly sliced

¼ cup cilantro roots

1 clove garlic

½ tsp coriander, ground

½ tsp caraway seed, ground

½ tbsp fish sauce

¼ tsp shrimp paste (optional)

2 tbsp oil

■ Combine all the ingredients in a
food processor and process until
smooth.

Boar Jus

1½ quarts boar stock

½ bunch cilantro

4 cloves star anise

½ ounce dried galanga root

½ stalk lemon grass

1 shallot

1 lime leaf

1 ounce ginger, sliced

1 tbsp sweet butter

Place boar stock, cilantro, star anise,
galanga root, lemon grass, shallot, lime
leaf, and sliced ginger in a heavy stock
pot. Bring stock and all ingredients to
a boil, and reduce by half. Strain stock
and return liquid to heat, then reduce
again by half. When reduced, stir in
whole sweet butter over medium heat
until dissolved. Set aside in a warm
place.

For Simplicity's Sake:

The rich and nutty boar blends well with the Asian accent of this dish. The paste will
make an excellent crust, but not everyone will have access to lemon grass and cilantro
roots. Check with an Oriental market for these ingredients. If you can't obtain them,
use stems of cilantro and lemon zest. Fish sauce is found in most supermarkets and
Oriental markets. Shrimp paste is listed as optional, but if you happen to have cleaned
shrimps on hand, puree them until they form a paste and you'll have a great addition.
To prepare boar or game stock, see "Basic Recipes."

Wild Boar Adobo and Grilled Venison Sausage with Coconut Mango Compote

Submitted by K.D. MacEachron • Thornapple Village Inn • Ada, Michigan   *Serves Four*

Wild Boar Adobo

1 bay leaf
4 cloves garlic, minced
½ cup white wine vinegar
pinch kosher salt
2½ pounds wild boar rump cut, cubed
½ cup water
4 tbsp olive oil
3 tbsp soy sauce
1½ cups tomato, deseeded, diced
3 tbsp coriander, chopped

■ Combine bay leaf, garlic, vinegar, kosher salt, wild boar, and water in a sauce pan. Bring to boil, stirring well, and simmer for about 20 minutes until meat is tender. Strain, reserving the cooking liquid and the meat separately. Sauté the meat in olive oil until golden brown, then add reserved cooking liquid. Simmer for five minutes, then add soy sauce, tomatoes, and coriander. Continue cooking until heated through.

Coconut Mango Compote

½ cup raisins
½ cup light rum
4 peeled mangos, deseeded and diced ½"
salt and pepper to taste
2 tbsp butter
1½ tbsp garlic, minced
1 cup brown sugar
1 tsp allspice
1 tsp cumin seed, toasted
2 tbsp orange zest
¼ cup fresh ginger, chopped
1½ cups coconut

■ Soak raisins in the rum for one hour. Season the diced mangos with salt and pepper. Melt butter in a sauce pan, then add mangos and garlic. Cook for two minutes, then add brown sugar, allspice, cumin, orange zest, and ginger. Cook for five minutes longer, then add coconut and raisins with the rum. Bring to boil and let simmer for five minutes. Let cool.

To serve: Serve wild boar adobo over rice and garnish with compote and grilled venison sausage (optional).

For Simplicity's Sake:

This recipe showcases the versatility of the firm, red boar meat by using a stewing method. You can serve this with venison sausage and rice. If fresh mango is not available use jarred mango or plums.

Wild Boar Namekagon with Port Lemon Sauce

Provided by Christopher P. Ray • Flat Creek Eatery and Saloon • Hayward, Wisconsin   *Serves Four*

Wild Boar

1½ pound boar loin, cleaned and trimmed
2 tbsp roast pecans, chopped
2 cloves garlic, sliced thin
6 ounces Spiced Fruit Chutney
salt and pepper to taste
¼ tsp olive oil

■ Butterfly the wild boar loin, being sure not to cut all the way through the meat. Pound loin out to 1/4" thickness with a meat hammer. Lay flat and spread the spiced fruit chutney (below), covering all but a 1/4" lip along the meat's outer edges. Sprinkle roast pecans over the chutney.

■ Lay sliced garlic over the chutney, spreading evenly throughout. Sprinkle lightly with salt and pepper. Roll the boar into a roulade, jelly roll style, and brush lightly with olive oil. Wrap tightly in a sheet of foil, twisting both ends of foil to ensure tight closure. Bake in a 350° oven for approximately 20 minutes or until firm to touch. Let rest for five minutes before removing from foil.

Port Lemon Sauce

1½ cups port wine, red
2 tbsp garlic, chopped
1 tbsp shallot, chopped
1 cup chicken stock
2 cups game stock
¼ tsp dried thyme
¼ tsp allspice, ground
½ lemon zest of
½ lemon, juice of
⅛ tsp white pepper
1 tbsp corn starch slurry
pinch salt

■ In a sauce pan, reduce the garlic and shallot with port wine by three-quarters. Add chicken and game stocks. While simmering, add remaining ingredients except for the corn starch slurry. After ten minutes, add slurry and simmer for ten more minutes or until starch taste has cooked out. Blend in a food processor, strain, and set aside.

Spiced Fruit Chutney

¾ cup dried pear, julienned
1 cup dried apples, julienned
¾ cup dried apricot, julienned
½ cup dried pineapple, julienned
½ cup raisins, golden or regular
2½ cups spiced rum (Captain Morgan's or other)
32 ounces Major Grey's chutney
1 tsp nutmeg, ground

■ Soak all dried fruits in rum overnight. Strain, reserving rum and fruits separately. Mix the fruit well with Major Grey's chutney and nutmeg. Add a shot of rum if too thick.

To serve: Place port lemon sauce on half of the plate. Slice the wild boar roulade and shingle four slices over the sauce.

For Simplicity's Sake:

A dish named after the Namekagon River, which flows through Wisconsin's northwoods. Food and many other trade goods were transported via this lively river. My recipe combines dried fruits and nuts, giving the chutney a sweetness that complements the smooth sauce. A shock of lemon brings the whole thing together. To prepare game stock, chicken stock, or cornstarch slurry, see "Basic Recipes."

Black Hills Bison Roulade
served with Indian Fry Bread and Wojapi

Submitted by T. Gregson • Laughing Water Restaurant • Crazy Horse, South Dakota   *Serves Six*

Bison

3 pounds boneless bison, sliced very thin

⅓ cup onion, minced

⅓ cup dijon mustard

3 bacon strips

6 dill pickle spears

▉ Slice the bison extremely thin, then lay it in six flat, smooth piles. Brush each pile with dijon mustard and sprinkle with onion. Add half a strip of bacon and place a pickle spear in the middle of each pile. Roll meat tightly around the pickles, then braise on a hot grill or sauté pan to seal. Place in baking dish, add chicken stock, and bake for three hours at 300°.

Indian Fry Bread Medallions

4 cups flour

1 tbsp baking powder

1½ tsp salt

1½ tsp cooking oil

water

▉ Sift the flour, baking soda, and salt. Add the oil and enough water to make a soft dough. Coat your hands with flour and knead until the dough has some spring. Shape into small balls and pat each ball into a flat cake. Keep patting and stretching the dough into a thin sheet. Fry each round of dough in very hot oil, turning once, until puffy and golden.

Wojapi (Sauce for Fry Bread)

12 ounces fresh, frozen, or canned chokecherry juice

2 tbsp fresh honey

corn starch

▉ Put the chokecherry juice in a small pan. Bring it to a boil and sweeten with honey to taste. Add corn starch slurry to thicken until it reaches syrup consistency. Drizzle over the top of the fry bread.

To serve: Slice meat down center. Serve with fry bread and sauce.

For Simplicity's Sake:

This is called "Pah-ha-sah-pah Pte-hcha-kay" in the native tongue, and it's served with a traditional fry bread. Wojapi sauce is made with chokecherries, but you can use any of your favorite berries—or even peaches or plums.

Grilled Mexican Spiced Buffalo Skirt Steak
with Duck and Smoked Jack Enchilada, Molé Sauce and Jicama Slaw

Submitted by Bryan C. Previte • Country Club of Darien • Darien, Connecticut   *Serves Two*

Grilled Mexican Spiced Buffalo

1 12-ounce buffalo skirt steak,
    cleaned and trimmed
2 cloves garlic, minced
2 tbsp lemon juice
salt and pepper to taste
Mexican spice mixture (equal parts
    paprika, cumin, coriander,
    cayenne and allspice) to taste
¼ cup olive oil

■ Combine all ingredients and marinate the buffalo skirt steak for up to two hours. Grill or broil to desired temperature. Medium rare (120° internal temperature) is suggested.

Duck and Smoked Jack Cheese Enchilada

1 6-inch corn tortilla
⅓ cup smoked Monterey Jack cheese,
    shredded
¾ cup duck leg meat, shredded
vegetable oil

■ Combine the duck and cheese together. Heat oil in a sauté pan, then dip tortilla in and out to soften, not to fry. Roll duck and cheese mixture up in tortilla and bake in 350° oven for 10 minutes.

Molé Sauce

2 tomatoes, deseeded and chopped
2 cups chicken stock
¼ cup chocolate
2 tbsp tomato paste
1 medium onion, chopped
7 dried ancho chiles, toasted
2 tbsp peanut butter
1 tsp cinnamon, ground
1 tsp paprika
sesame seeds

■ Sauté onions in a sauté pan until they are translucent. Add the tomatoes and chiles and sweat for two minutes until the moisture begins to seep out, then add the remaining ingredients. Simmer for 15 minutes, puree in food processor, and strain, setting aside the sauce. Garnish with sesame seeds.

Jicama Slaw

1 cup jicama, julienned
2 tbsp black beans, cooked
2 tbsp corn, blanched
1 tsp fresh cilantro, chopped
1 tbsp olive oil
½ cup yellow bell pepper, julienned
½ cup red bell pepper, julienned
pinch sugar
juice of one lime
tabasco sauce to taste

■ Combine all the ingredients in a bowl.

To serve: Place a portion of the skirt steak on each plate. Cut the enchilada in half and place half on each plate. Serve the jicama slaw on the side. The molé sauce can be poured over the tail of the skirt steak or served on the side.

For Simplicity's Sake:

Southwestern and Mexican foods seem to attract one another, and the attraction is a blessing for those who relish delicious foods. Molé sauce is defined in our glossary. Jicama, "the Mexican potato" makes a refreshing salad ingredient. When you're using cilantro, avoid using too much!! If you overindulge, the cilantro will add a soapy flavor to your food. Dried ancho chiles have become much easier to find. Look for them at your supermarket or a specialty store.

Buffalo Sirloin with Whiskey Onion Marmalade

served with Wild Mushroom Strudel, and Quinoa and Dried Cherry Pilaf

Submitted by Martin Wolf, C.E.C. • Waterman Village ARA • Mt. Dora, Florida   *Serves Four*

Buffalo

4 6-ounce buffalo sirloin steaks,
   1 inch thick
2 cups yellow onion, diced
4 tbsp black pepper, ground
¼ cup butter
½ cup Jack Daniels (or other good
   bourbon)

■ Prepare the strudel and pilaf (right) first. When ready to cook the meat, coat the steaks with black pepper and grill to medium rare. At the same time, sauté the onions in butter until they are translucent. Place the steaks in the pan with the onions, then pour in the whiskey. Finish cooking steaks to medium rare (120° to 130°) or desired doneness.

Wild Mushroom Strudel

½ pound wild mushrooms (shiitakes
   or morels), sliced
½ pound domestic mushrooms,
   sliced
2 tbsp butter
¼ cup armagnac or brandy
2 tbsp bread crumbs
2 tbsp shallots, diced
salt to taste
2 sheets fillo dough

■ Clean and slice the mushrooms. Sauté them with the shallots until the mushrooms are tender. Add enough bread crumbs to soak up excess moisture. Add the brandy, and sauté briefly.

■ Lay out the fillo, being careful not to let it dry out, and brush with melted butter. Place one sheet of fillo on top of the other. Position the mushroom mixture on one end and roll up. Brush with butter and bake in a 375° oven until golden brown. Cut into four pieces.

Quinoa Pilaf

1 cup quinoa
3 cups water
1 tsp garlic, chopped
½ cup dried cherries
¼ cup pine nuts
1 tbsp olive oil

■ Sauté the garlic in the olive oil, then add the quinoa and brown. Add the water and simmer until it is absorbed and the quinoa is tender. Add cherries and pine nuts, remove from heat, and let it stand for 30 minutes.

To serve: Serve the sirloin steaks with the whiskey onion marmalade poured over the tail piece of each steak. Add the pilaf and a roll of mushroom strudel. Flame when served by igniting the liquor with a match, being careful to hold the pan away from your body.

For Simplicity's Sake:

Whiskey onion marmalade adds kick to the full-flavored sirloin. Wild mushroom strudel is good, but buffalo can also stand on its own. Quinoa gives an interesting twist to the pilaf. To work with filo dough, see Chef Bill Aschenbrenner's recipe for venison strudel.

Roast Buffalo Tenderloin with Cranberry Chipotle Barbecue Sauce

Submitted by Robert Macey • 1776 Restaurant • Crystal Lake, Illinois   *Serves Four*

Buffalo Tenderloin

1 buffalo tenderloin, cleaned and trimmed

1 pound apple wood bacon, sliced

1 caul fat (stomach lining)

■ Wrap the tenderloin in the bacon and caul fat. Roast the tenderloin in a 400° oven until medium rare or 120° internal temperature.

Cranberry Chipotle Barbecue Sauce

4 chipotle peppers, deseeded and diced

1 onion, diced

1 red bell pepper, diced

1 bottle dark beer

2 cloves garlic, minced

1 cup brown sugar

1½ cups cider vinegar

½ cup tomato paste

¼ cup molasses

4 cups cranberries

■ Combine all ingredients and simmer in a sauce pan for 20 minutes. Remove from heat and puree.

To serve: Slice buffalo and serve with sauce.

For Simplicity's Sake:

Another simple presentation, demonstrating that the great flavor of buffalo needs little help. The combination of dark beer, cranberries, and chipotle peppers creates a unique barbecue sauce. Caul fat (see glossary) is optional. You might use toothpicks instead in order to secure the bacon. Cranberries can be dried, fresh, frozen, or even canned. Chipotle peppers are smoked, dried jalapenos.

Caribou with Dark Ale Brandy Mushroom Glaze
served with Wild Rice and Grains, Snow Cap Beans, and Shiitake Mushrooms

Submitted by Keith Elfering • Airport Hilton • Minneapolis-St. Paul, Minnesota   *Serves Two*

Caribou

2 7-ounce loins of caribou, cleaned
    and trimmed
olive oil
seasoning salt

■ Cut the tenderloins into 1-1/2-ounce medallions. Place plastic wrap over the medallions and pound lightly with a meat hammer. Rub the medallions with olive oil and sprinkle with seasoning salt. Grill or broil the caribou medallions briefly to medium rare.

Dark Ale Brandy Mushroom Glaze

1 cup dark ale
¼ cup brandy
½ cup mushroom broth
½ tbsp brown sugar
1 tbsp fresh rosemary, chopped
½ tsp sage
· pinch seasoning salt

■ Combine all the glaze ingredients in a sauce pan and reduce by half. Keep the sauce warm until served.

Wild Rice Mixture

2 tbsp wheatberries, cooked
2 tbsp wild rice, cooked
2 tbsp barley, cooked
2 tbsp lentils, cooked

■ Sauté the wheatberries, wild rice, lentils and barley with the dark ale glaze and reduce.

Vegetable Mixture

2 tbsp snow cap beans, cleaned and
    trimmed
2 shiitake mushrooms, sliced
½ cup carrots, julienned
½ cup sweet corn

■ Sauté the vegetables in the dark ale glaze until warm.

To serve: Place the vegetable mixture in the middle of the plate, add the wild rice mixture, and fan the caribou medallions out, overlapping the vegetable mixture. Drizzle with the remaining dark ale glaze.

For Simplicity's Sake:

Dark ale and brandy, combined with shiitake mushrooms, bring out the ultimate in this fine-grained meat, which is prized for its flavor. Wheatberries add a nice, nutty element. I suggest soaking the berries overnight before cooking, which helps them expand and cook much more easily. If you're not in the mood to use all the grains and lentils, substitute wild or plain white rice.

Medallions of Caribou Loin
with Idaho Huckleberry Butter Sauce

Submitted by Christian Berg • Shore Lodge Hotel • McCall, Idaho   *Serves Four*

Marinade

2 tbsp salad oil
⅓ cup soy sauce
¾ cup pineapple juice, canned
⅓ cup sherry
8 cloves garlic, chopped
¼ cup fresh ginger, chopped
¼ bunch fresh chives, chopped

▪ Mix all ingredients well. Marinate caribou loin overnight.

Idaho Huckleberry Sauce

¼ cup fresh huckleberries, washed
1½ cups burgundy
2 cups game stock or beef stock
½ cup sugar
1 rosemary sprig
1 bay leaf
½ tsp black pepper, cracked
½ cup cold butter chunks

▪ In a sauté pan, reduce all ingredients except whole butter by three-quarters. Remove from heat and slowly whisk in the cold butter chunks until all have blended. Strain and add the huckleberries.

Caribou Loin

1 2-pound caribou loin, cleaned and trimmed
3 slices bacon
salt and pepper to taste

▪ Brown all sides of the caribou loin in a very hot sauté pan. Place the loin in a roasting pan and set the slices of bacon on top of the roast, then finish in a 325° oven. Roast for 12 to 15 minutes or until an internal temperature of 120° is reached. Remove from oven and let rest for 10 to 15 minutes before slicing into 1/2-inch medallions.

To serve: Pour the huckleberry sauce on the plate, and fan the medallions over the sauce.

For Simplicity's Sake:

The marinade uses relatively little oil, and the smooth, rich sauce lets the fine taste of caribou speak for itself. You can substitute lingonberries, blueberries, or your favorite berry for the huckleberries. See "Basic Recipes" for the game or beef stock.

Medallions of Elk Tenderloin
with Wild Rice Pancake and Smokey Corn Sauce

Submitted by David Timney • Balaban's • St. Louis, Missouri   *Serves Four*

Elk Tenderloin Medallions

1 16-ounce elk tenderloin, cleaned
   and trimmed

■ Slice tenderloin into two-ounce medallions. Grill or broil the medallions to desired temperature. They will cook very quickly, because they are so small.

Wild Rice Pancake

2 cups wild rice, cooked
1 red bell pepper, diced
1 green bell pepper, diced
2 green onions, chopped
2 eggs
⅓ cup milk
salt and pepper to taste
1 tsp baking powder
½ cup all-purpose flour

■ Mix all the ingredients together and fold until thoroughly combined at the consistency of batter. Cook the wild rice pancakes in a sauté pan, browning both sides. Set aside.

Smokey Corn Sauce

1 cup corn kernels, smoked
3 cups veal stock
2 cups heavy cream
¼ cup tomato paste
1 tbsp brown sugar
1 tbsp worcestershire sauce
2 cups barbecue sauce
1 tsp garlic powder
½ tsp tabasco sauce
½ tsp black pepper
¼ cup sweet sherry

■ Combine all ingredients and heat them in a sauce pan. Reduce by half, then puree and strain through a strainer.

To serve: Place the elk medallions on top of the wild rice pancake, and pour the sauce around the pancake.

For Simplicity's Sake:

The corn and wild rice take us back to the earliest foods that were cooked with venison. The flavor of the elk needs no help whatsoever. You'll love the use of barbecue sauce in the smokey corn sauce. You can substitute chicken stock for the veal stock (see "Basic Recipes").

Grilled Elk Chops
with Buffalo Mozzarella and Foie Gras

Submitted by Richard Billingham • L'Apogee Ltd. • Steamboat Springs, Colorado   *Serves Four*

Elk Chops

4 6-ounce elk chops, cleaned and
    trimmed
2 ounces olive oil
black pepper, ground
4 2-ounce slices buffalo mozzarella

Sun-Dried Tomato Demi-glace

2 ounces olive oil
4 2-ounce foie gras, sliced
1 tsp shallots, chopped
12 sun-dried tomatoes, rehydrated
3 ounces cognac
8 ounces brown sauce
salt and pepper to taste

■ To make the demi-glace, heat olive oil in a sauce pan over moderate heat, then add the foie gras. Sauté until just warm, remove foie gras and set it aside. Add shallots and the sun-dried tomatoes to the same pan and sauté for a few minutes. Add the cognac and reduce the liquor out. Now add the brown sauce and simmer until the sauce coats the back of a wooden spoon.

■ To make the chops, rub them with olive oil and sprinkle with black pepper. Grill on an outdoor barbecue or an inside gas grill until medium rare (120° internal temperature). When done, place a slice of mozzarella on each chop and warm in an oven. Top each chop with a slice of foie gras, then the sauce.

To serve: The meat can be served atop wild rice pancakes.

For Simplicity's Sake:

Elk has long been considered a superior meat, and it can serve as a substitute for any red meat on the grill. An Italian chef once told me, "Fresh mozzarella is the silver, but fresh *buffalo* mozzarella is the gold." Tomatoes, dried or fresh, are the finest complement to mozzarella. See Basic Recipes for preparation of the brown sauce or veal stock. You can consider the foie gras optional.

Arctic Musk Ox
with Red Onion Confit and Shiitake Mushrooms

Submitted by Peter Zang • Dick's Bar • Hudson, Wisconsin   *Serves Four*

Musk Ox Tenderloin

4 five-ounce musk ox tenderloins, center cut

2 tbsp olive oil

2 tbsp fresh thyme, chopped

1 tsp juniper berries, crushed

■ Season the tenderloin with salt and pepper and juniper berries. Sear tenderloins on all sides in a hot pan. Place in 375° oven until medium rare (120° internal temperature). Remove from oven and let meat rest for five minutes.

Mushrooms

1 quart veal demi-glace (brown stock)

¼ cup red currant jelly

½ cup shiitake mushrooms, sliced

2 tbsp butter

■ Reduce the demi-glace (brown sauce) and red currant jelly in a sauce pan until it heavily coats the back of a wooden spoon. Sauté the shiitake mushrooms in butter and add to the sauce. Set aside.

Red Onion Confit

2 cups red onions

½ ounce butter

½ cup port wine

■ Sauté the onions in butter until transparent. Add port wine and reduce until the pan is dry, stirring onions occasionally.

Vegetables

1 carrot, peeled and sliced ¼" thick

4 asparagus spears, each cut into six pieces

1 tbsp butter

4 thyme sprigs (optional)

■ Steam the vegetables until tender.

To serve: Place red onion confit in center of plate. Ladle the sauce around the confit. Slice the steaks in half and place them atop the confit. Distribute the steamed vegetables around outside lip of the plate, and add a sprig of thyme atop the meat.

For Simplicity's Sake:

Go figure. Musk ox is an excellent, top-ranking game meat, yet it's still hard to come by. Juniper berries are a delightful addition to almost any game meat. To crush the berries, simply place them between two sheets of wax paper and roll them with a rolling pin. See "Basic Recipes" for a demi-glace recipe. For the red onion confit, julienne thin slices of red onion and sauté until thoroughly cooked.

Braised Rubbed Venison Loin
with Smoked Chestnuts and Barley

Submitted by Jeffrey Kurfuss • Brook and Company • Morrrisville, Pennsylvania   *Serves Four*

1 boneless venison loin, cleaned and
    trimmed

Beaujolais Boysenberry Jus
1 gallon game stock or brown sauce
1 cup beaujolais
4 shallots
1 pint boysenberries
salt to taste
pepper to taste

■ Reduce the stock or brown sauce by
half in a large pot. In a separate sauce
pan, reduce the beaujolais wine,
shallots, and boysenberries to a dry
consistency. Add the reduced stock,
and reduce to a thick, syrup-like
consistency. Season to taste with salt
and pepper and strain.

Stuffing
½ bag hickory wood chips
4 tbsp vegetable oil
1 pound chestnuts
½ loaf white bread, finely diced
2 pounds pearl barley
1 Spanish onion, finely diced
5 stalks celery, finely diced
salt and pepper to taste
sage to taste
thyme to taste

■ Use a Weber grill (or similar) with
hickory wood chips. Ignite and let
smolder. Put the chestnuts on the grill
and smoke them for approximately 75
minutes, then remove from the heat
and let cool. Heat olive oil with diced
onions and sprigs of thyme in a pot.
Add the pearl barley and coat in oil.
Add venison stock until it just covers
the barley, then cook in a 350° oven
until the liquid is gone.

■ Sauté the onions, celery, and sage.
Then chop the chestnuts and fold
them in with the fully cooked barley.
Fold in the diced bread until the
stuffing binds together, and season
with salt and pepper.

■ Butterfly the venison loin. Season
with salt and pepper, then fill with
stuffing. Tie the venison loin closed
with butcher string for searing.

Rub
2 cloves elephant garlic, roasted
1 bunch fresh sage, chopped
salt and pepper to taste
1 cup olive oil

■ To finish, mix the ingredients for
the rub in a large bowl, then coat the
venison loin completely with the rub.
Heat oil and sear the venison loin on
all sides to a dark golden brown. In a
350° oven, cook the venison loin to an
internal temperature of 120° (about
35 minutes). Remove the meat and
brush on the remaining rub. Turn the
oven down to 300° and continue
cooking the venison until it reaches
140° internally. Remove the meat, let
it rest for about 20 minutes, then slice
into 1/2" thick medallions.

To serve: Fan medallions onto the
plate and drizzle with sauce. Serve
with wild rice and red lentil pilaf.

For Simplicity's Sake:
A traditional treatment of venison incorporating the lost art of cooking with
chestnuts and barley. Contrary to popular belief, barley is not just grown for
beer! You can roast the chestnuts in your oven, but it's a treat to smoke them.
If you wish, you can substitute blueberries or blackberries for boysenberries.
Game stock or brown sauce can be used (see recipe in glossary). Be sure you
don't cut all the way through the meat when you butterfly the loin.

Broiled Red Venison Shortloin with Wild Cranberry and Morel Sauce

Submitted by John D. Flach • Buck's T–4 Lodge • Big Sky, Montana   *Serves Two*

2 7-ounce red venison shortloins
½ cup dried morel mushrooms
½ cup wild cranberries
1 quart port wine
1 quart cranberry juice
1 cup cranberry vinegar
1 gallon game stock or brown sauce

■ Soak the morels and cranberries in port wine and cranberry juice until the morels are rehydrated. Heat the port wine, cranberry juice, cranberry vinegar, morels, and cranberries until reduced by one-half. Strain out the morels and cranberries and set them aside.

■ Add the liquid back to the pot with the game stock. Reduce by 1/3, then thicken with corn starch slurry to a medium consistency. Adjust the cranberry flavor if desired by adding more juice or vinegar.

■ Broil the steak to proper doneness. An internal temperature of 120° (medium rare) is suggested.

To serve: Place the desired amount of sauce on a plate. Place the steak on the sauce, and garnish with morels and wild cranberries.

For Simplicity's Sake:

A nice use of an alternative cut of meat. Using cranberries with game is an age-old (and not very well-kept) secret. Apple cider vinegar can be substituted for cranberry vinegar, and the dried mushrooms can be of the inexpensive boletus variety. Game or brown sauce can be used.

Pepper-Glazed Venison Loin with Sesame Crust and Mandarin Plum Sauce

Submitted by Mark Spelman • Camino Real Hotel • El Paso, Texas   *Serves Four*

1 venison loin, boneless and trimmed

Marinade

⅛ cup black pepper, coarse
2 tsp fresh garlic, minced
2 tsp wasabi powder
2 tsp Dijon mustard
¼ cup Chinese plum sauce
½ cup Worcestershire sauce
¼ cup soy sauce

▩ Combine the marinade ingredients. Place the venison into the marinade, pressing firmly on all sides so the pepper sticks to the meat. Marinate for two hours, covered and refrigerated.

To Complete the Dish

¼ cup peanut oil
½ cup dry sherry
1 cup venison or beef stock
1 cup sesame seed, toasted
½ cup Chinese plum sauce

▩ In a hot sauté pan, heat the peanut oil, then sear the meat on all sides. Add 1/4 cup of sherry and reduce by half. Add the marinade and the venison or beef stock while maintaining high heat. Keep turning the meat in the sauce, which will become very dark and syrup-like. When the meat has become completely glazed, remove it from the pan and let the meat rest for ten minutes on the counter. The meat should be medium rare at this point. Next, roll the glazed loin in the sesame seeds to coat.

▩ Finally, combine the plum sauce and 1/4 cup of sherry as a sauce to accompany the meat.

To serve: Slice the tenderloin at 1/4" to 1/2" thickness. Fan the slices on plate, pour the sauce over them, and complement with your favorite vegetable and wild rice.

For Simplicity's Sake:

Here, we bring American and Oriental cuisine together in an elegant fashion. It's a perfect example of how wild game lends itself to many cultural accents. Chinese plum sauce is found in the specialty sections of most supermarkets. Wasabi is a horseradish root powder commonly used in Japanese cuisine. If necessary, you can substitute prepared horseradish (same quantity) in the marinade. To toast the sesame seeds, simply place them on a sheet pan in a 350° oven until they're golden brown.

Cold Marinated Venison Salad with Roasted Roma Tomatoes and Fried Orange Rings

Submitted by Kraig Lundblad • Interlocken Country Club • Edina, Minnesota   *Serves Four*

Venison
1 24-ounce venison tenderloin, cleaned and trimmed

Marinade
½ cup orange juice
¼ cup soy sauce
¼ cup sherry
¼ cup extra virgin olive oil
2 cloves garlic, minced
1 tsp sugar
½ tsp ginger

■ Pierce the tenderloin with a fork and place it in a pan. Mix all the marinade ingredients and pour the mixture over the tenderloin. Cover and refrigerate for at least three hours. When ready, remove the tenderloin from the marinade and roast in a 350° oven until medium rare (internal temperature of 120°). Refrigerate until chilled, then slice.

Sautéed Cabbages and Fennel
1 medium red cabbage, julienned
1 medium green cabbage, julienned
5 medium fennel bulbs, julienned
6 tbsp extra virgin olive oil
salt and pepper to taste

■ Sauté the cabbage and fennel in separate pans, adding garlic and oil to both. Cook until tender. Refrigerate in separate containers or on separate plates.

Orange Vinaigrette
1 shallot, finely minced
1 tsp orange zest, minced
½ tsp salt
½ tsp tabasco sauce
1 tsp dijon mustard
3 tablespoons orange juice, frozen concentrate
3 tablespoons champagne wine vinegar
9 tablespoons extra virgin olive oil

■ Combine all the ingredients in a mixing bowl except the olive oil. Once combined, slowly whisk in the olive oil. Adjust the flavor to taste with orange juice concentrate or sugar.

Grand Marnier-Scented Fried Orange Rings
4 oranges, sliced ¼" thick
1 cup Grand Marnier

■ Remove the flesh, keeping the orange rind circles intact. Marinate in Grand Marnier for least 24 hours. Just before serving, fry briefly in a hot frying pan with oil. Be sure to fry both sides. Remove the rings and place them on a paper towel.

Roasted Roma Tomatoes
4 tbsp extra virgin olive oil
6 roma tomatoes, cut in half

■ Drizzle the tomatoes with olive oil, then roast at 350° for approximately 15 minutes or until the skins split. Set aside at room temperature.

To serve: Place cabbage and fennel on a plate. Stuff the greens through the orange rings, then stand the greens up in the center of the cabbage. Fan the sliced venison around the cabbage and fennel. Drizzle with vinaigrette and garnish with roma tomatoes and (if desired) honey-roasted cashews.

For Simplicity's Sake:
Cooked and chilled, venison is a real treat. You can roast garden tomatoes or use them fresh. The fennel and cabbage are a natural match, and the orange vinaigrette is a refreshing complement. You can use white wine vinegar in this recipe if you wish. Give the fried orange rings a try.

Hazelnut Crusted Red Venison Loin Stuffed with Chanterelle

Submitted by Guy Logan • Hillcrest Golf and Country Club • Altoona, Wisconsin   *Serves Six*

Rabbit Loins

4 rabbit loins, cleaned and trimmed

½ cup chanterelle dust

1 cup virgin olive oil

■ Be sure all silver skin is trimmed off. Marinate the cleaned meat in olive oil for 2 to 4 hours. Then place the loins on baking pan in a 350° oven for 10 minutes or until just done. When loins have cooled, remove excess oil and coat them well with chanterelle dust. Place in cooler until later.

To serve: Slice venison loin into 1/4" to 1/2" medallions. Fan four medallions over each plate and drizzle with sauce. Serve with vegetable and wild rice pilaf.

Red Venison Loin

1 5- to 7-pound red venison loin, cleaned and trimmed

2 quarts roasted hazelnuts, finely minced

■ Make sure all silver skin is removed from the meat. Butterfly the loin lengthwise, being sure to not cut all the way through the meat. Retrieve rabbit loins from cooler and trim the ends, so they butt up against each other to form one long loin. Place the rabbit loins on one end of the venison loin lengthwise, and roll them up as tightly as possible. Roll venison loin in the minced hazelnut. Place the loin on a baking pan and bake for 20 to 30 minutes or until medium rare. Let the roast cool about 10 minutes before slicing.

Morel Pink Peppercorn Sauce

2 tbsp whole butter

1 quart brown sauce (or venison stock)

½ cup pink peppercorns

1 quart morel mushrooms, small

1 cup Marsala wine

1 tbsp thyme, minced

2 cloves garlic, minced

½ cup arrowroot

■ Sauté the morels with butter, peppercorns, thyme, and garlic. Add the Marsala wine and reduce by half. Add 3 cups of the brown sauce (or venison stock) and reduce by two-thirds. Mix the remaining stock with arrowroot and slowly add this mixture to the sauce in the pan until slightly thickened.

For Simplicity's Sake:

This recipe provides more evidence of the ways in which game meats can complement one another. Mushroom dusts have become more popular. If your specialty store doesn't carry them, you can make your own out of dried chanterelle or other mushrooms. Simply puree the mushrooms in a food processor until dusty, then sift. Don't bring liquids to a boil after you've added arrowroot. This thickening agent does not hold up well under high heat. Morel farms now provide these delicious mushrooms to many specialty stores. See our "Basic Recipes" section for a brown sauce recipe.

Pan-Seared Maple Venison Chops with Root Vegetable Ragout

Provided by Christopher P. Ray • Flat Creek Eatery and Saloon • Hayward, Wisconsin   *Serves Four*

Venison Chops

8 4-ounce venison chops, French cut
1 cup pure maple or maple-flavored
  syrup
¼ cup kosher salt
salt and pepper to taste

■ Combine kosher salt, maple, and cold water. Soak the venison chops for one hour, making sure that all chops are totally submerged. Remove chops from the mixture and pat them dry. Season with salt and pepper. Sear the chops in a very hot skillet, browning both sides. Remove from pan when the meat is medium rare (120° internal temperature).

Root Vegetable Ragout

¼ cup pancetta, ham
2 tbsp olive oil
¼ cup carrots, finely diced
¼ cup onions, finely diced
¼ cup celery root, finely diced
¼ cup jicama, finely diced
1 tbsp horseradish root, grated
1 tbsp garlic, minced
1 tbsp juniper berries, crushed
1 tsp chili powder
4 cups brown sauce
2 tbsp parsley, chopped
salt and pepper to taste

■ Brown the pancetta in a sauté pan, then remove from pan and strain. Wipe the pan, add olive oil, and heat. Add carrots and onion, and sauté for five minutes over medium heat. Add celery root and jicama, and sauté for three more minutes. Add horseradish root, garlic, juniper berries, and chili powder, and stir well. Cover with brown sauce and bring to boil, then reduce heat to simmer. Simmer until vegetables are al dente (firm in the center). Remove from heat, add parsley, and season with salt and pepper. Set aside until served.

To serve: Stir the ragout well and spoon the mixture onto a round plate until covered. Place venison chops on the ragout, crossing the bones at the top of the plate.

For Simplicity's Sake:

A simple presentation utilizing a brine, as our forefathers did. You won't need a knife when you sit down to eat. Pancetta adds flavor and aroma. It's primarily used as a flavor base in Italian cooking for pasta sauces, stews, roasts, and vegetable dishes.

Roasted Colorado Venison Roulade

Submitted by Jack W. MacMurray III • The Sonnenalp Resort • Vail, Colorado   *Serves Four*

Venison

3 venison tenderloins, cleaned and trimmed

▨ Trim all the silver skin off the tenderloins. Butterfly each loin, but don't cut all the way through the meat. Pound out with a meat hammer to approximately 1/4" thickness and set aside.

▨ To stuff, lay the meat out flat and spread the stuffing mixture over each tenderloin, leaving 1/2" uncovered around the outside edges. Roll tightly, jelly roll style.

▨ Sear all sides in a hot skillet with oil, then remove. Rub with dijon rub (below), coating thoroughly but not too thickly. Finish in a 450° oven for approximately 8 to 12 minutes.

Dijon Rub

1 cup Grey Poupon mustard
3 tbsp shallots, minced
3 tbsp fresh rosemary, minced
2 tbsp kosher salt
1 tbsp black pepper, fresh ground

▨ Thoroughly combine all ingredients, then set aside.

Stuffing

1 pound blanched spinach, drained and minced
12 ounces smoked Wisconsin cheddar, shredded
¾ cup shiitake mushrooms, destemmed and finely chopped
6 slices wheat bread, ¼" diced
½ cup pistachios, toasted and chopped
2 egg yolks

▨ Spinach should be totally drained, containing no water. Combine all ingredients thoroughly.

Sauce

1 tbsp butter
1 tbsp shallots, minced
1 cup tawny port wine
¾ cup venison glacé or brown sauce
2 tbsp butter, room temperature

▨ Heat butter in a sauté pan and sweat the shallots for one minute. Add the tawny port and reduce by half. Add glacé or brown sauce and reduce again by half. Whip in the butter just before service.

To serve: Slice venison tenderloin 1/4" to 1/2" thick. Fan the slices on plate, with each medallion overlapping. Drizzle sauce over medallions.

For Simplicity's Sake:

I remember using a dijon rub on racks of lamb and receiving many compliments. The stuffing is filled with simple, earthy flavors to complement the rich, smooth sauce. To toast pistachios, shell them and place them on a sheet tray in a 350-degree oven until they're golden brown and aromatic. For brown sauce or game stock, see "Basic Recipes."

Roasted Loin of Venison with Bacon/Molasses Dressing Served with Scallion Spoonbread

Submitted by Nicholas Petti • Cafe Trio • Chapel Hill, North Carolina   *Serves Four*

Venison

4 7-ounce pieces venison loin,
   cleaned and trimmed
black pepper, coarse
salt
fresh garlic, minced

■ Rub venison with pepper, salt, and garlic. Sear on all sides and roast to medium rare (120° internal temperature). Let rest, then slice thinly.

Bacon/Molasses Dressing

¼ pound bacon, chopped
1 clove fresh garlic, minced
½ tsp fresh thyme, chopped
1 tbsp fresh chives, chopped
¼ cup cider vinegar
2 tbsp molasses
¼ cup olive oil
salt and pepper to taste

■ Sauté bacon, garlic, and herbs. Brown the bacon. Deglaze the pan with vinegar, and stir in molasses. Whisk in the olive oil and adjust seasoning. Keep warm.

Scallion Spoonbread

2½ cups milk
1 cup yellow cornmeal
3 ounces butter
1 tsp salt
1½ tsp baking powder
3 eggs, separated
1 bunch scallions (green onions),
   chopped

■ Heat milk to boiling point, add cornmeal, and cook on low heat for ten minutes. Remove from heat, then add butter, salt, and baking powder, mixing well. Add egg yolks and scallions, stirring until smooth. Whip egg whites to soft peaks and fold into cornmeal mix, using a wooden spoon. Place the mix in a greased muffin or loaf pan and bake in a 350° oven for 25 to 35 minutes. Bread is done if toothpick inserted in the bread comes out dry.

To serve: Place the spoonbread in center of the plate. Pour dressing around the spoonbread and arrange the venison slices over the dressing. Serve with fresh vegetables.

For Simplicity's Sake:

Chef Petti shows us how effective a straightforward combination of flavors can be with the "game meats." The spoonbread is a fun touch, and it's easy to make.

Roasted Venison with Wild Mushroom Stuffing and Cranberry Robert Sauce

Submitted by Ray Hollingsworth • Loon River Cafe • Sterling Heights, Michigan   *Serves Four*

Venison with Wild Mushroom Stuffing

½ pound venison for grinding, trimmed
1½ pound venison, top round
1 egg white
1 cup heavy cream
1 cup wild mushroom mix
4 tbsp onion, chopped
⅓ cup cabernet sauvignon
½ tsp fresh garlic, minced
3 juniper berries, crushed
pinch salt and pepper

■ Cut the venison top round with the grain, removing a piece about ten inches long and five inches wide. Pound out with a meat hammer to approximately 1/4" thickness. Sprinkle with a dash of wine and salt and pepper.

■ Take the mushroom mix and run it through a food processor until it is finely chopped. Then place the onions and mushrooms in a sauté pan and heat until the moisture is gone. When done, remove from the heat and let cool.

■ Place the ground venison, egg whites, cream, and seasoning in the food processor and blend. When blended, remove from the bowl and mix in the mushrooms. Grill one side of the pounded-out venison, then remove from heat. Set the venison on a long piece of foil, grilled side down. Place the stuffing on the edge of the grilled meat, then roll into a roulade, wrapping it tightly in the foil. Roast in a 350° oven for 30 minutes, or until an internal temperature of 155° has been achieved.

Cranberry Robert Sauce

¼ cup cranberries
1 cup port wine
2 tbsp shallots, chopped
1 tsp dry mustard
2 tbsp powdered sugar
½ cup brown sauce

■ Place the wine, cranberries, shallots, and mustard in a saucepan. Reduce by half. Remove from heat and add the brown sauce and sugar. Run through a strainer, then set aside.

To serve: Cut venison in 1/4" slices or into 2" pieces at an angle. The latter will create a tower effect when you stand the meat up on its flat end. Serve on a bed of sauce with braised or grilled vegetables.

For Simplicity's Sake:

There are many recipes that combine game meats and fowl, but here is a combination of two types of venison. By grinding venison to fill the roulade, the chef is allowing the venison flavor to shine through, while exhibiting two textures. Cranberry Robert sauce could complement any number of game dishes. To prepare brown sauce, see "Basic Recipes."

Tropical Spiced Venison with Gorgonzola Sauce
served with Roasted Walnut-Barley Pilaf and Wilted Greens

Submitted by Tom Hommes • Wayzata Country Club • Wayzata, Minnesota   *Serves Four*

Venison
24-ounce venison loin, cleaned and
   trimmed

Marinade
1 tbsp sesame seeds, toasted
12 peppercorns, toasted
20 coriander seeds, toasted
5 cloves, toasted
3 juniper berries, toasted
½ cinnamon stick, toasted
1 bay leaf
1 tsp kosher salt
1 tsp sugar
2 tbsp butter

■ Toast the first six ingredients in a 350° oven until sesame seeds are golden brown. Place between two sheets of wax paper and use rolling pin to grind the toasted spices together with bay leaf, salt, and sugar until well pulverized. Rub soft butter on the venison loin, then coat with spices, cover, and refrigerate for two hours. When ready to cook, sear the venison in a very hot pan, then roast in a 375° oven until medium rare (internal temperature of 120°).

Gorgonzola Sauce
2 quarts venison stock (or beef
   stock)
1½ cups port wine
6 ounces butter
6 tbsp shallots, minced
8 ounces gorgonzola cheese

■ In a sauce pan, add two tbsp butter and minced shallots. Sauté shallots for one minute, then add 3/4 cup of port wine. Bring to a boil and add stock. Bring to desired consistency (should thoroughly coat the back of a wooden spoon). Add remaining 3/4 cup of port wine and whip in four tbsp whole butter. Sprinkle cheese over the sauce when ready to serve.

Barley Pilaf
2 cups barley
4 cups water
½ cup carrots, minced
1 red bell pepper, minced
4 tbsp red onion, minced
12 ounces walnuts, roasted
1 tbsp olive oil
salt and pepper to taste

■ Cook barley in water until tender, then strain and rinse. Toss barley in oil and season. Add vegetables and nuts, and serve warm.

Wilted Greens
1 bunch Swiss chard, julienned
1 head radicchio, julienned
1 bunch arugula, julienned
1 tbsp olive oil
⅓ cup white wine
lemon pepper to taste

■ Heat oil in sauté pan, then add greens. Deglaze with wine and season.

For Simplicity's Sake:
There's no truer marriage of flavors than matching a quality gorgonzola with a fine port wine. The recipe also makes excellent use of a Caribbean-accented, dry rub marinade. To crush seeds, you might instead place them between two sheets of waxpaper and crush with a rolling pin. Toast the seeds as you would roast nuts (in a 350-degree oven until golden brown). Wilting these bitter greens removes some of the bite and completely changes the texture of the dish. For the game stock (or possibly chicken stock), see "Basic Recipes."

Venison Ragout "After the Hunt Supper"

Submitted by Thomas M. Chulick • Rolling Rock Club • Ligonier, Pennsylvania

Serves Four

1 pound venison round, 1" cubes
6 tbsp whole butter
salt and white pepper to taste
½ red onion, minced
3 cloves garlic, minced
2 cups morel mushrooms, sliced
1 tbsp parsley, chopped
1 tbsp thyme, chopped
1 sprig rosemary, chopped
4 tbsp flour
⅓ cup dry sherry
¼ cup burgundy
½ cup venison stock
4 russet potatoes, quartered
1 sweet potato, sliced ¼" thick
2 carrots, sliced
½ pound fresh frozen spring peas

■ Sauté venison until brown in two tbsp of butter. Season with salt and white pepper. Remove the meat. Add 4 tbsp butter and sauté the onion, garlic, morels, and herbs briefly. Add flour to make a medium roux (thickener). Add sherry and burgundy while stirring, and heat through. Add venison stock, bring to boil, and reduce to simmer for three minutes. Add potatoes, sweet potato, and carrots. Return meat to pan and bring to simmer until vegetables are nearly done. Add peas, then cook until vegetables are done.

To serve: Serve over a bed of your favorite rice or pasta.

For Simplicity's Sake:

Here's a nice alternative to roasting a round of venison, based on wild game cooking traditions. The pan is yours, so add any vegetables you enjoy—possibly even grains or legumes.

Venison Strudel

Submitted by William T. Aschenbrenner, C.E.C./A.A.C. • The Mar-a-Lago Club • Palm Beach, Florida
1993 COMPETITION FINALIST   *Serves Six*

Venison Strudel

2 venison, Denver leg, 12 ounces
    each, cleaned and trimmed
¾ cup roasted Macadamia nuts,
    chopped fine
4 fillo sheets

1½ cups vegetable medley (beets,
    carrots, turnip), angel hair and
    julienned
assorted fresh herbs
salt and pepper

12 new potatoes, quartered and
    steamed

■ Make sure venison is cleaned and
free of silver skin. Roll venison in
ground nuts and wrap in fillo. Bake in
the oven for 17 minutes at 375°. Sauté
vegetables with fresh herbs and season
to taste.

Port Wine Sauce

½ cup veal stock
½ cup six-grape port wine
1 tbsp brown sugar
⅛ cup red vinegar
¼ ounce cornstarch
1 tbsp butter

■ Melt the butter in a pan. Add the
brown sugar and melt, then deglaze
with the vinegar. Add three-quarters of
the port wine and simmer, then add
the veal stock. Dissolve the cornstarch
in the remaining port wine. Add to
sauce as a thickening agent.

To serve: Serve a five-ounce portion
of venison strudel in the center of the
plate, surrounded by assorted
vegetables and potato laced with port
wine sauce.

For Simplicity's Sake:

Chef Aschenbrenner makes a nice dish look and taste magnificent. It's an excellent use of the
Denver cut, combined with macadamia nuts. You'll want to keep the paper-thin fillo dough
moist, important, so it doesn't break up or crumble. To do this, place a moist paper towel on
a counter. Cover it with a sheet of plastic wrap, place the fillo sheets on the wrap, and cover
the sheets with another layer of plastic wrap. Place a second moist paper towel on top. Work
with one piece of the fillo dough at a time, and lightly oil each sheet as you use it.

Wild Game Chili with Black Beans
served with Jalapeno Corn Muffins

Submitted by Gloria Ciccarone-Nehls • The Big Four Restaurant, Huntington Hotel • San Francisco   *Serves 10 to 12*

Wild Game Chili

½ cup cooking oil
4 yellow onions, diced medium
6 jalapeno peppers, deseeded and
   fine diced
3 tbsp chili powder
2 tbsp cumin, ground
1 tbsp thyme, dried
1 tsp oregano, dried
1 tsp celery seed
1 tsp paprika
½ tsp black pepper
½ tsp anise seed
½ tsp cayenne
pinch ground cloves
4 bay leaves
4 pounds wild game meat (venison,
   antelope, rabbit, elk, duck, or
   game sausage), ground or cubed
2 cups red chili sauce
1 quart beef stock or beef broth
5 cups black beans, cooked, or
   2½ cups uncooked (optional)

In a large pot, sauté onion and peppers in oil over medium heat until soft. Add spices and sauté for several minutes longer. Add meat and cook until lightly browned. Add chili sauce and bring pot to a boil. Add enough beef broth to barely cover the ingredients and bring to boil again. Lower heat and simmer for 2-1/2 to 3 hours, stirring every half hour. Add beans, and season to taste with salt and pepper. Garnish with grated sharp cheddar or jack cheese and chopped red onion.

Jalapeno Corn Muffins

1 cup flour
1 tsp baking soda
1½ tsp baking powder
1 tbsp sugar
1 tsp salt
¾ cup yellow cornmeal
1½ cups buttermilk
2 eggs
4 tbsp melted butter
2 jalapeno peppers, deseeded and
   fine diced

Preheat oven to 425°. Sift flour, baking soda, baking powder, sugar and salt together. Add cornmeal. In a separate bowl, combine buttermilk, eggs, butter, and pepper. Combine liquid and dry ingredients. Pour into small-sized, buttered muffin tins and bake for 12 to 15 minutes.

To serve: Serve chili in an appropriate bowl with warm muffins.

For Simplicity's Sake:

One of America's great game chefs showcases her diversity by combining a variety of game meats in this fabulous chili, then complementing it with her jalapeno corn muffins. See "Basic Recipes" for beef stock or bouillon. I encourage you to go for the black beans, but you're not limited to these meat and sausage combinations.

Crispy Fried Rattlesnake and Rabbit Paupiette
served with Red Pepper Corn Bread, and Braised Cactus and Peppers

Submitted by Craig D. Bash • Normandy Restaurant • Denver, Colorado   *Serves Four*

Crispy Fried Rattlesnake

½ pound rattlesnake, boneless
¼ cup cornmeal
1 tsp salt and white pepper
1 tbsp herbs (combine chervil,
    parsley, thyme, sage and chives)
¼ cup flour
¼ cup egg wash

▪ Blend cornmeal, herbs, salt, and white pepper in a food processor until the mixture becomes green. Dip the rattlesnake in the flour, then the eggwash, then the cornmeal mixture.

▪ Heat 1/2" of oil in a frying pan until extremely hot, then fry the breaded rattlesnake, browning all sides. Remove and pat dry on paper towel.

Rabbit Paupiette

1 pound rabbit meat, ground
1 cup heavy cream
1 egg, whole
1 egg white
pinch salt
⅛ cup sage, chopped
2 rabbit loins

▪ Put the ground rabbit in a food processor and mix thoroughly with heavy cream. Add the egg, the egg white, and salt, then mix (do not overmix). Remove and place in a bowl, then fold in the sage. Lay the ground meat out on a piece of plastic wrap. Place the rabbit loins in the center of the ground meat, wrapping tightly so the loin is coated thoroughly with the ground mixture.

▪ Poach in water approximately 20 to 25 minutes, making sure the rabbit is totally submerged. Remove from the water and set aside.

Red Pepper Corn Bread

1 cup cornmeal
1 cup flour
¼ cup sugar
1 tbsp baking powder
½ tsp salt
2 eggs
4 tbsp butter, melted
1 cup milk
1 red bell pepper, diced
½ yellow bell pepper, diced

▪ Combine all dry ingredients, sifting everything except the cornmeal. Sauté the red and yellow peppers together, seasoning lightly, until the peppers are warmed through. Let the peppers cool to room temperature. Warm the milk and butter together, then whisk in the eggs until thoroughly combined. Mix the milk mixture with the dry mixture until thoroughly moist, but do not overmix. In a greased muffin or loaf pan, bake in a 400° oven for 30 to 40 minutes. Check doneness with a toothpick. Corn bread is done when the toothpick comes out dry. Remove from oven and let it cool.

Braised Cactus And Peppers

1 pound cactus (nopales), cleaned
    and quartered

½ red bell pepper, diced

2 tbsp white vinegar

½ cup chicken stock

½ haberno pepper, deseeded and
    minced

4 tbsp butter

salt and pepper to taste

   Blanch the cactus in boiling water, then shock in cold water to cool. Sauté the bell peppers together. Add the cactus and sauté briefly. Add the white wine vinegar and simmer for one minute. Add chicken stock (or water) and let simmer until the stock is nearly gone. Finish by adding the butter and seasoning. When removed from heat, it's ready to serve.

Sauce

1 ounce rattlesnake trimmings,
    seasoned and floured

2 tbsp shallots, minced

2 tbsp carrots, diced

1 cup port wine

½ gallon brown sauce

1 bouquet garni (combine sage,
    thyme, bay leaf, and pepper)

2 tbsp sage, chopped

   Brown the rattlesnake trimmings in a sauce pot, then remove. Sauté shallots and carrots in the same pot, then add port wine and reduce until it's almost dry. Add the bouquet garni and the brown sauce, and reduce by half. Strain through a strainer and add the liquid to the rattlesnake trimmings and sage.

To serve: Remove the plastic wrap from the rabbit and cut the meat in slices 1/2-inch thick. Place the braised cactus on a plate with the cornbread. Fan out the slices of rabbit and place the fried rattlesnake on the plate. Drizzle the rabbit and rattlesnake with sauce.

For Simplicity's Sake:

Another combination of two meats. If you can't locate rattlesnake, try the rabbit as an entree. You can buy the rabbit already ground or try rabbit sausage. Use rabbit scraps for the sauce. This is a great cornbread, and for something different, try roasting the bell peppers. Be sure that your cactus is well-cleaned.

North American Spice-Rubbed Rabbit Saddle

Submitted by Jerry L. Snider • Hyde Park Cafe • Cleveland, Ohio   *Serves Two*

Rabbit Saddle

1 8-ounce rabbit saddle, boneless
   and trimmed
1 red onion, sliced
1 cup oyster mushrooms, sliced
1 cup spinach, cleaned and trimmed
salt and pepper to taste

■ Marinate the rabbit for about two hours in a shallow pan with one-half of the chile oil, half of the red onion, and salt and pepper. Remove rabbit from the marinade and rub it with spice mix. Sear all sides of rabbit in hot pan with remaining chile oil. Finish rabbit in a 450° oven with the mushrooms and red onions, and cook until medium to medium well. Just before the rabbit is finished roasting, add spinach to the pan.

Spice Mix

1 tbsp maple sugar
1 tsp thyme, minced
½ tsp salt
1 tbsp dry mustard
1 tbsp dried mint
2 tbsp paprika
½ tsp cayenne pepper
1 tsp pepper, ground
1 tsp juniper berries, ground

■ Mix all ingredients well.

Chile Oil

2 cups canola oil
1 tsp fresh garlic, chopped
1 tsp tomato paste
¼ cup dried red chiles
½ tsp salt
1 tsp crushed red pepper
1 tsp black peppercorn

■ The chile oil can be prepared days in advance. To prepare, sauté garlic, dried chiles, red pepper flakes, and 1/2 cup canola oil in a sauté pan until the garlic is brown. Add salt, tomato paste, and peppercorn, leaving on heat for one minute more. Let cool, then add the rest of the ingredients. Set aside in a cool, out of the way area. Caution: Chile oil can burn sensitive skin.

Dried Roma Tomatoes

3 roma tomatoes
1 tsp rosemary, chopped
salt and pepper to taste

■ The roma tomatoes can also be prepared ahead of time. First, cut the tomatoes in half. Sprinkle them with chopped rosemary and salt and pepper. Place them skin-side down on a sheet tray and dry them in a 120° to 140° oven for 2 to 3 hours, until they are half of their original size. Remove from the oven and set aside at room temperature.

To serve: Remove from the oven and serve with roasted vegetables and dried roma tomatoes.

For Simplicity's Sake:

You can probably find chile oil or a similar item at your grocery store. If not, make your own and store it for a multitude of uses. Be extremely careful when working with hot oil. The rub is spectacular here, and the pan roasting makes this a very tender dish.

Pistachio-Crusted Loin of Rabbit
with Foie Gras Spaetzle and Wild Mushroom Pockets

Submitted by Scott Uehlein • Los Abrigados Resort and Spa • Sedona, Arizona   *Serves Four*

Rabbit Loin

1 rabbit loin, cleaned and trimmed
½ cup pistachio nuts, ground
1 tbsp butter
salt and pepper to taste

■ Dust the rabbit loin with salt and pepper, then bread the loin with pistachios. In a hot sauté pan with butter, brown all sides of the rabbit. Finish in a 350° oven until firm. Meanwhile, lightly brown the spaetzle in the same sauté pan and season with salt and pepper. Warm the mushroom pockets in the oven if necessary.

Sauce

1 cup orange muscat wine
½ cup verjus
1 cup game stock or brown sauce
¼ cup whole butter, softened

■ Reduce the wine and verjus by three-quarters. Add the stock or brown sauce and cook for about five minutes until thick. Just prior to service, whisk in the butter and season with salt and pepper.

Mushroom Pockets

4 radicchio leaves, poached in verjus
3 tbsp shallots, chopped
¼ cup whole butter
8 oyster mushrooms, julienned
8 shiitake mushrooms, destemmed and julienned
3 tbsp pistachios, ground
¼ cup game stock or brown sauce
¼ cup cilantro, chopped

■ Sauté the shallots in butter until they become transparent. Add mushrooms and sauté for three minutes. Add pistachios, game stock (brown sauce), and cilantro. Cook until almost dry. Season with salt and pepper. Fold the mushroom mixture into radicchio cups and set aside.

Spaetzle

1 ounce foie gras scraps
1 cup water
3 eggs
2 cups bread flour
salt and pepper to taste

■ Puree the foie gras with the water. Pour into a bowl, then add eggs and salt and pepper. Whisk the flour in slowly until the consistency of cake batter is achieved. Pass the batter through a large-holed colander and into boiling salted water. Cook for 30 seconds and shock spaetzle in ice water. Toss in oil as you would pasta (to prevent sticking) and set aside.

To serve: Rabbit can be sliced or served whole, sitting atop of spatzle. Drizzle the sauce over the rabbit and serve the mushroom pockets as an accompaniment.

For Simplicity's Sake:

This creative rabbit presentation was selected as one of our original finalists in 1995, but unfortunately Chef Scott couldn't make the trip. The spaetzle is unique in its use of foie gras, and the sauce is simply wonderful. If you take your time with the mushroom pockets and the rabbit, you'll have a heavenly meal.

Wheatberry, Gorgonzola and Herb-Stuffed Saddle of Rabbit with Dried Cranberry Chutney

Submitted by Bryan C. Previte • Country Club of Darien • Darien, Connecticut   *Serves Two*

1 rabbit saddle, boneless and
    trimmed
salt and pepper to taste
3 bacon slices

Stuffing

3 tbsp wheatberries, cooked
2 tbsp herbs (chervil, tarragon, and
    thyme), chopped
4 ounces rabbit trimmings, pureed
¼ cup gorgonzola cheese
2 tbsp brandy

Sauce

2 tsp fresh garlic, minced
2 tbsp shallots, minced
⅔ cup oyster mushrooms
½ cup vermouth
1 cup chicken stock

■ Season rabbit with salt and pepper. Fold cheese, wheatberries, herbs, and brandy with the meat puree. Stuff the rabbit saddle with the stuffing mixture, and fold flaps of meat over to encase. Wrap two bacon slices across the saddle and wrap one slice lengthwise. Place rabbit saddle in a sauté pan and put pan in a 400° oven for 15 to 20 minutes. Remove from the oven and take meat out of pan. Wipe the pan clean and add shallots, garlic, and mushrooms. Deglaze with vermouth, add stock, and reduce on stovetop by half. Whip in two tbsp of whole butter to finish the sauce (demi-glace). Remove bacon from rabbit before serving.

Dried Cranberry Chutney

½ cup dried cranberries
¼ cup raisins, golden or regular
1 cup port wine
pinch cayenne pepper
¼ cup pears, diced
½ cup cider vinegar
2 tbsp walnuts, chopped
2 tsp arrowroot

■ Combine all ingredients in a sauce pan and bring to a simmer for 15 to 20 minutes

To serve: Slice rabbit and serve on chutney.

For Simplicity's Sake:

The nutty flavor of wheatberries and fresh herbs gently influences the mild, delicate rabbit, and using the pan to make the sauce helps the meat retain its natural flavor. The cranberry chutney works as an attractive garnish. Arrowroot is a thickening agent (see glossary).

Wild Rabbit Casserole

Submitted by Andy Emrisko • Outdoors Inn • Cleveland, Ohio

Serves Four

Wild Rabbit Casserole

2 rabbits, cleaned and trimmed

2 quarts water

1 pound cauliflower, broccoli, and carrot mix, cleaned and washed

½ pound brussel sprouts, cleaned and washed

1 26-ounce can cream of mushroom soup

1½ cups wild rice, washed

4 tbsp butter or margarine

1 tsp salt

1 cup mozzarella cheese, shredded

■ Cook rabbits in boiling, salted water until tender. Remove from water and let cool, setting the water aside for stock. If using frozen vegetables, thaw. Pull all meat from rabbit, return the bones to the reserved water, and reduce by half. Mix the rabbit with wild rice, two cups of rabbit stock, cream of mushroom soup, and butter. Place in cassserole dish, cover, and bake in 325° oven until three-quarters of the liquid is gone. Then add the vegetable mix and brussel sprouts, cover, and finish baking in the oven until the rice is fully cooked. Remove cover and sprinkle mozzarella cheese on casserole. Return to oven long enough to let the cheese melt or brown.

Curry Roasted Onion and Duckling Cakes with Dried Blueberry Vinaigrette

Submitted by Randy Reynolds • Pfister Hotel • Milwaukee, Wisconsin   *Serves Four*

Duck Cakes

2 mallard duck breasts

2 yellow onions, peeled and
   quartered

2 tbsp curry powder

salt and pepper to taste

1 tbsp olive oil

3 tbsp butter, melted

■ Roast the duck breasts, fat side up, in a 250° oven until the meat is easily pulled apart. Allow to cool enough so the meat can be handled, then coarse-shred it with a knife, discarding the fat. Set the meat aside.

■ Separate the layers of the onion quarters, toss with oil and curry, and roast in a 375° oven until well-browned and cooked through. Let them cool and coarse-shred them with a knife. Combine duck and onions in a bowl and season, then set aside.

■ Heat butter in a sauté pan. Pat the duck mixture into eight small cakes, sauté in butter until both sides are golden brown and heated through. Drain on paper towels.

Dried Blueberry Vinaigrette

½ cup dried blueberries

1 tsp juniper berries

3 cloves

1 cinnamon stick

½ vanilla bean

4 black peppercorns

pinch nutmeg

1 clove garlic

½ cup dry red wine

½ cup duck stock

¼ cup balsamic vinegar

¾ cup olive oil

salt to taste

■ Combine the first ten ingredients in a sauce pan and reduce to approximately 1/2 cup. Strain into a clean sauce pan, then reduce the liquid to a syrup consistency. Add vinegar, oil, and salt, then whisk to combine. Remove from heat and set aside.

To serve: Drizzle vinaigrette over duckling cakes. This serves well with chilled greens and/or fresh vegetables, and you can also garnish it with fresh berries.

For Simplicity's Sake:

You can serve these as the main entree with vegetables, cooked or chilled, or try the cakes on a salad. Blueberries are a natural complement to the duck. You can substitute fresh or frozen for the dried fruits. Specialty spice stores and some groceries will carry the vanilla bean. You can remove the breast meat from a whole duck, and make duck stock from the remains, or purchase the duck breast by itself and substitute chicken stock for the duck stock.

Espresso Duck Breast
served with Braised Cabbage and Matchstick Potatoes

Submitted by Nicholas Petti • Cafe Trio • Chapel Hill, North Carolina   *Serves Four*

Duck

4 6-ounce duck breasts, cleaned and trimmed

■ See marinating instructions below before cooking. Sear the breasts, meat side down, in a hot pan. Turn over, reduce heat to low and cook, pouring off rendered fat as necessary. When the skin is crisp, remove meat from pan. Slice it thinly.

Marinade

½ cup brewed espresso
1 tsp salt
½ tsp sugar
1 tsp unsweetened cocoa powder

■ Combine all the marinade ingredients and marinate the duck breasts overnight.

Braised Cabbage

½ head green cabbage, cored and quartered
¼ cup dried apricots, diced
⅓ cup dry white wine
½ tsp vanilla extract
salt and pepper

■ Combine the ingredients in a large, hot pan. Cover and braise until tender.

Matchstick Potatoes

1 large russet potato, julienned
vegetable oil or olive oil

■ Pour one-half inch of oil into a hot skillet. Fry the julienned potato until golden brown, then remove and let it rest on a paper towel.

To serve: Place cabbage in center of plate and arrange the sliced duck around the cabbage. Garnish with the matchstick potatoes.

For Simplicity's Sake:

This will get you up and about. The duck meat marries well with this dark, heavy marinade. Cabbage lends itself well to a good many game meats and birds. Most grocery stores and supermarkets now carry dried fruits. Dried cranberries or cherries would also work well with the cabbage and duck.

Jeckyl Island Duck

Submitted by Michael E. DiMarco, C.C. • Snooters Galley and Pub • Belle Vernon, Pennsylvania   *Serves Four*

Roasted Duck

2 whole ducks, cleaned
2 cups honey
2 tbsp peanut butter
salt and white pepper to taste
1 bunch chives
2 cups peanuts, finely chopped
2 cups ginger snap crumbs
6 Vidalia onions, finely julienned

Preheat oven to 375°. Toss half of julienned onions in a small amount of oil and season with salt and white pepper. Fill the duck cavity with seasoned onions. Rub the duck skin with salt and white pepper. Place on roasting rack in roasting pan and put in oven for approximately for 1-1/2 hours.

While duck is in the oven, place peanuts in a food processor and chop them finely but not to a powder. Repeat the process with the ginger snaps, then combine with the peanuts and set aside.

Remove duck from the oven and set aside to cool. Strain and reserve the grease. Split the duck and remove the skin in four large pieces without rupturing. Remove the breast, leg, and thigh meat from the carcass halves. Cut the skin pieces into pentagonal shapes. Place the meat from the duck on the skin pieces, and fold them over the meat in the shape of envelopes. Coat the envelopes with honey and the peanut mixture, and flash them in the oven until the peanuts are browned. Remove from oven. Flash the duck envelopes once more in the oven just before serving.

Vidalia Onion Peach Jam

4 Vidalia onions, finely julienned
2 pounds hickory chips
12 Georgia sweet peaches
4 tbsp apricot preserves

Peel and pit the peaches. Cut them into sixths, then coat them lightly with oil. Roast in a 375° oven for five minutes. Place two tbsp of duck fat in a small sauce pan and sweat the rest of the onions along with the peaches. When the peaches are soft and warmed through, add the rest of the honey and apricot preserves, simmer, and remove from heat.

Stewed Tomatoes

2 plum tomatoes, skinned and
  seeded
4 ounces duck fat
salt and white pepper to taste

Place a small amount of the duck fat in a sauce pan and stew the tomatoes over medium heat, adjusting to taste with salt, white pepper, and lemon juice. When tomatoes are tender, remove from heat.

To serve: Spoon a portion of peach onion jam on the plate, then place a duck envelope atop the jam. Drizzle with jam. Garnish with whole and chopped chives and stewed tomatoes.

For Simplicity's Sake:

This dish combines unusual use of the skin with a very interesting crust and jam. There are those who say there is no substitute for the Vidalia, but if you must, try a Walla Walla sweet, a Colossal, or another sweet onion. Peaches that do not come directly from Georgia may be permissible.

Pan-Roasted Duck Breast with Cranberry Applejack Glaze

Submitted by Ron Berg • Gunflint Lodge • Grand Marais, Minnesota   *Serves Four*

Pan-Roasted Duck Breast

4 boneless duck breasts, halved
salt and pepper to taste
¼ cup applejack brandy
4 ounces Cranberry Glaze

■ Use a knife to cut diagonal slashes about 1/4-inch apart on the fat side of the duck, being careful not to cut into the meat. Season the duck breasts with salt and freshly ground black pepper. Sauté the breasts fat-side down over medium heat, pouring out the fat as it accumulates, until the skin is nicely browned. Pour out any remaining fat and turn the duck breasts skin-side up. Pour four tablespoons of the applejack brandy over the duck breasts. Remove the duck breasts to a roasting pan and finish in a 400° oven until medium rare to medium—5 to 10 minutes. Remove from oven and keep them warm.

■ To finish the sauce, use remaining applejack with the liquids from the roasting pan. Heat in a sauce pan and reduce until syrupy. Add 1/2 cup of the cranberry glaze, including some of the cranberries, and heat to a simmer.

Candied Cranberries / Syrup

1 cup sugar
¼ cup water
1 cup raw cranberries, washed

■ Cook sugar and water over low heat, stirring until the sugar dissolves. Combine this syrup with cranberries in a double boiler. Cover and place over simmering water. Cook for 45 minutes, stirring occasionally. Remove and let stand at room temperature for one to eight hours. Strain, holding the cranberries and the syrup separately. Makes about 1/2 cup of syrup.

Cranberry, Orange, and Wine Mixture

½ cup raw cranberries, washed
1 orange, zest and juice only
½ cup game or chicken stock
¼ cup red wine
½ tsp ground black pepper
½ tsp cayenne pepper
¼ cup Madeira wine
⅓ cup port wine

■ Simmer cranberries with orange juice and zest until the skins burst on the cranberries. Combine the cranberry-orange mixture with remaining ingredients in a food processor and puree. Strain and discard the pulp. Return the liquid to a sauce pan and bring to simmer. Cook for five minutes to combine flavors.

Cranberry Glaze

■ To make the cranberry glaze, combine the syrup with the cranberry-orange-wine mixture (1/2 cup syrup to 1-1/2 cups mixture), and bring to a simmer. Make a cornstarch slurry and use as needed to thicken the mixture until it reaches the consistency of heavy cream. Stir in the reserved cranberries, then set aside.

To serve: Slice the duck diagonally and fan slices on a plate. Spoon the sauce and cranberries over the duck.

For Simplicity's Sake:

The sauce complements the duck beautifully. Cherries or blueberries would work as well. To make the zest, use a potato peeler or cheese grater to remove the rind. Peel off the rind only, because the white pith will taste bitter. See "Basic Recipes" to prepare the cornstarch slurry.

Raspberry Marinated Duck Breast Stuffed with Chevre and Wild Rice, Wrapped in Puff Pastry and Served with Raspberry and Kiwi Coulis

Submitted by Christopher Camp • Lamouille Area Vo Tech • Newport, Vermont   *Serves Four*

Marinade

½ cup raspberries
½ cup white vinegar
1 tsp tarragon
½ cup olive oil
1 tbsp sugar

◼ Puree the raspberries and sugar in a blender. Pass through a strainer and place in bowl. Add vinegar, tarragon, and olive oil to the bowl and mix thoroughly. Set aside.

Duck

2 8-ounce duck breasts
salt and pepper to taste
10 ounces chevre goat cheese
1 cup wild rice, cooked
1 tsp tarragon
½ cup onion, finely chopped
½ cup celery, finely chopped
1 cup flour
½ cup vegetable oil
2 sheets puff pastry shells
2 eggs
¼ cup water
½ cup fresh raspberries (for garnish)
½ cup fresh blueberries
1 kiwi, sliced (for garnish)

◼ Take the two duck breasts and cut into four half breasts. Pound out the breasts with a meat hammer to 1/2" thickness. Add the breasts to the marinade and let set for one hour.

◼ Sauté the onion and celery until al dente (firm in center), then set aside to cool in a bowl.

◼ Add broken-up chevre cheese, wild rice, blueberries, and tarragon to bowl and mix together thoroughly.

◼ Remove breasts from marinade. Place approximately 1/4 cup of stuffing mixture in center of each duck breast cavity and push thumb in middle. Place one raspberry in each indentation. Wrap breasts around stuffing, roll them in flour, and shake off excess flour.

◼ Heat up a sauté pan with vegetable oil, put the duck in, and brown it evenly, first searing each seam to seal the stuffing inside. After about four to five minutes, remove the duck from pan and let cool.

◼ When cooled, place each duck breast in the center of a puff pastry. Wrap together, trim off the excess pastry, and seal with an egg wash made from egg yolk and water. Set in refrigerator. Pre-heat oven to 450° and place duck in the oven, cooking for 12 to 15 minutes or until evenly browned. Remove from oven and set aside for five minutes.

Raspberry Coulis

1½ cups raspberries
½ cup sugar
¼ cup lemon juice

◼ Puree raspberries, sugar, and lemon juice in a blender. Pass through a strainer and set in refrigerator.

Kiwi Coulis

3 kiwi fruits, peeled and chopped
3 tbsp sugar
¼ cup lemon juice

◼ Puree kiwi, sugar, and lemon juice in a blender. Pass through a strainer and set in refrigerator.

To serve: Take duck in pastry and cut diagonally in half. Place raspberry coulis on one side of the duck and garnish with kiwi slices. Place the kiwi coulis on the other side of the duck and garnish with additional kiwi and raspberries.

Fowl Delight

Submitted by Leeroy Villers, C.C. • Westin Hotel • Boston, Massachusetts *Serves Four*

Fowl

3 quail, 2 grouse, and 1 pheasant,
  boneless
3 eggs
3 cups cream
6 tbsp butter
salt and pepper to taste

■ Slice the breast meat of all birds thinly. Lay them seperately between plastic wrap layers and pound to an even thickness.

Pheasant Garniture

1 cup yellow and green bell peppers,
  deseeded and diced
2 tbsp pistachios, diced
1 tbsp chives
4 tbsp brandy
1 egg
1 cup cream
2 tbsp butter

Grouse Garniture

1 cup diced carrots
¼ cup asparagus
1 tbsp basil
¼ cup shiitake mushrooms
2 tbsp red onion
4 tbsp chardonnay
1 egg
1 cup cream
2 tbsp butter

Quail Garniture

½ cup red bell peppers, diced
1 tbsp truffles, sliced
2 tbsp port wine
1 egg
1 cup cream
2 tbsp butter

■ Coarsely chop the leg meat, scrap meats, and any livers that came with the birds. Separate into three equal portions. Make three separate batches of mousse as follows: Take one portion of meat plus garniture for pheasant and puree in a food processor to a stiff consistency. Repeat this process for meat plus grouse garniture, then meat plus quail garniture. Keep all three mousses separate.

■ Lay out a sheet of plastic wrap and return to the pounded meats. Spread a layer of the pheasant on the wrap, then spread a thin layer of the pheasant mousse; next spread a layer of the pounded grouse, followed by a layer of the grouse mousse. Finish with a layer of quail meat followed by the quail mousse. Roll the entire, layered mixture into a roulade. Wrap tightly into a cheesecloth or plastic wrap and poach in water until firm (20 to 25 minutes). When done, let it rest for ten minutes. Slice 1/4" to 1/2" thick and allocate three slices per person.

To serve: Serve with a mixture of sautéed carrots, zucchini, squash, turnip, red pepper, and yellow pepper.

For Simplicity's Sake:

If you have three different birds and some time on your hands, this recipe is a crowd-pleaser. The three mousses offer clean, simple flavors. See our glossary if you're unfamiliar with truffles.

Goose Breast Stuffed with Dried Blueberries, Cranberries, and Wild Boar Pancetta with Chardonnay Orange Sauce

Submitted by Britton Unkefer • Paper Valley Hotel • Appleton, Wisconsin   *Serves Four*

Goose

2 wing-on goose breasts, cleaned

■ Pound out the goose breasts with a meat hammer, skin side down, 1/4" thickness. Place approximately 1/4 cup of stuffing (previously prepared) in the middle of the breast. Fold sides of the breast over the stuffing, making sure one side overlaps the other. If necessary, tie with butcher string. Season with salt and pepper. In a hot sauté pan, sear all sides of the breasts. Finish in a 350° oven until the internal temperature is 150°.

Stuffing

2 shallots, julienned
1 cup dried blueberries
1 cup dried cranberries
1 cup wild boar pancetta (or regular pancetta), julienned
¼ cup chardonnay

■ Sauté the shallots in olive oil for one minute, then add blueberries and cranberries. When berries are warm, add chardonnay and reduce until dry. Remove from heat, then mix in the pancetta. Let cool.

Chardonnay Orange Sauce

2 shallots, diced
1 clove garlic, diced
½ small cantaloupe, diced
2 cups chardonnay
4 cups orange juice

■ Sauté the shallots and the garlic. Add the chardonnay, reduce by 1/2, then add the cantaloupe and orange juice. Simmer until the cantaloupe is very soft, then puree and strain through a fine strainer.

To serve: Cut breasts into servings of three or four slices each and fan out over the sauce. Alternately, cut each breast into two parts and serve over the sauce. Drizzle extra sauce over the meat before serving.

For Simplicity's Sake:

Goose is the big game bird among the waterfowl. This is one meat that needs to be cooked thoroughly, all the way through, but be careful not to dry the meat out. A fruit stuffing laced with the flavor of pancetta allows you to go wild with options, and bacon or ham can replace the pancetta. Cantaloupe adds a different twist and a great thickening agent to the sauce.

Braised Roulade of Goose Breast with Mushroom Sauce

Submitted by Brian J. Moran • The Milwaukee Club • Milwaukee, Wisconsin   *Serves Four*

Goose Roulade

1 16-ounce goose breast, skin removed

2 ounces fresh spinach, cleaned & trimmed

3 ounces chanterelle mushrooms, diced

1 ounce smoked duck breast, diced

fresh sage leaves for garnish (optional)

■ Remove skin from goose breast. Pound the meat with a meat hammer to a thickness of 1/4 to 1/2 inch. Sauté the spinach lightly. Lay the goose breast out flat, skin side down, and spread the spinach evenly over the meat. Add the smoked duck breast and two tablespoons of diced mushrooms, spreading evenly. Roll the goose breast and place two toothpicks through the seam to keep it rolled tightly.

Braising Stock

1 quart chicken stock

1 cup port wine

¼ tsp sage

¼ tsp garlic

pinch of white pepper

pinch of dried thyme

■ Heat butter or oil in a sauté pan and brown the roulade on all sides, then remove it from the pan. Place the roulade in a roasting pan and add the chicken stock, port wine, and seasonings. Cover and place in a pre-heated oven at 375° for 1-1/2 hours or until tender. Remove the roulade from pan and keep it covered.

Mushroom Sauce

2 cups braising stock

mushrooms (remaining from roulade)

pepper to taste

thyme to taste

¼ cup heavy cream

■ Sauté the remaining mushrooms in butter until soft, then remove from the pan and save. Pour two cups of braising stock from the roasting pan into a sauce pan. Reduce it by one-half and thicken it slightly with a cornstarch slurry until it lightly coats the back of a wooden spoon. Add the sautéed mushrooms with the pepper, thyme, and heavy cream. Simmer for 15 minutes.

To serve: Slice the goose roulade into medallions. Place these on the plate and pour sauce over them. Garnish with sage leaves (optional). Best when served with wild rice.

For Simplicity's Sake:

Here you'll combine the flavor of two birds to achieve tremendous results. You can order duck pre-smoked or smoke the meat yourself. You might also substitute a favorite sausage. Cook the goose fully, but do not dry the bird out. See "Basic Recipes" for a chicken stock recipe.

Pan-Roasted Goose

with Stewed White Beans, Shallot Pudding, and Apple and Wild Rice Griddle Cakes

Submitted by Gregory Werry, C.W.C. • The Westin Hotel • Seattle, Washington •
1994 COMPETITION CHAMPION

Serves Eight

Goose Breast

4 boneless, 12-ounce goose breasts,
    trimmed
2 tbsp olive oil
½ tbsp garlic, minced
1 tbsp shallots, minced
1 tsp lavender, minced
kosher salt and white pepper to taste

■ Trim goose breasts, removing excessive skin, fat, and silver tendons. Score the skin with a sharp knife. Rub the flesh side of the breast with olive oil and seasonings. Allow to marinate for two to four hours.

■ To cook, sear the breasts skin-side down in a heavy sauté pan. Remove and discard fat (grease) as necessary. Allow the skin to become crisp, then turn over and finish cooking in a 350° oven for about eight minutes. Remove from the oven and allow to rest for five minutes before slicing.

Stewed White Beans with Boudin

¼ cup apple smoked bacon,
    julienned
2 tbsp onions, diced
1 tbsp celery, diced
1 tbsp carrot, diced
1½ tbsp tomato paste
¾ cup white beans
1½ pints chicken stock
1 cup pre-cooked boudin, cubed
salt and pepper to taste
juice of one lemon
2 tbsp fresh parsley, chopped
Sachet:
    1 bay leaf
    ½ tbsp black peppercorns
    ½ tbsp rosemary
    2 cloves garlic

■ Sauté the bacon until crisp. Add onion, celery, and carrot, and sauté until the onion is translucent. Add the tomato paste and dry beans, cooking five minutes to expand the flavor.

■ Add stock and sachet. Bring to a boil, then cover and remove from heat. Allow to set for one hour to tenderize beans. Then add more stock if needed and bring mixture back to a slow simmer. Cook until tender, about 1-1/2 hours. At the last moment, stir in the sliced boudin and chopped parsley, and adjust the seasoning.

Roasted Shallot Pudding

3 eggs, whole
12 ounces half and half
½ cup roasted shallots, pureed
1 tbsp rosemary
½ tbsp thyme
lemon juice to taste

■ Blend all ingredients together in mixer, then strain through a fine strainer. Spray the inside of a muffin pan with a non-stick spray. Bake in a water bath pan for 20 minutes at 300°. Keep warm.

Apple and Wild Rice Griddle Cakes

1 cup wild rice, cooked and cooled

1 cup white rice, cooked and cooled

1 Granny Smith apple, grated

½ cup pecans, toasted

2 tsp orange zest

½ tsp nutmeg

salt and pepper to taste

2 tbsp herbs (parsley, chives, rosemary), chopped

¼ cup flour

1 egg, lightly beaten

■ Combine all dry ingredients, tossing with flour to coat them evenly. Mix in the egg. Form into cakes and griddle-fry until golden brown on both sides.

To serve: Stand the shallot pudding up on the plate. Place two apple wild rice griddle cakes on the plate. Add the stewed white beans so they overlap the griddle cakes. Fan slices of goose breast over the stewed white beans.

For Simplicity's Sake:

A wonderfully wide array of flavors and ingredients. Cook the goose thoroughly, but don't dry out the meat. You may find lavender extract in specialty or health stores. Roast shallot pudding is a delicious, easy to make complement. To roast, peel the fresh shallot, coat it with olive oil, and place in a 350-degree oven on a sheet tray. When it becomes golden brown and aromatic, remove from pan and let it cool. For an explanation of the water bath, see our glossary. You might substitute andouille sausage for the boudin.

Cider-Braised Wild Grouse with Natural Sauce

Submitted by Michael DiMarco, C.C. • Snooters Galley and Pub • Belle Vernon, Pennsylvania   *Serves Four*

Cider-Braised Grouse

2 whole grouse
1 gallon apple cider
1 onion, finely diced
2 carrots, finely diced
4 ribs celery, finely diced
butter
salt and white pepper to taste
vegetable oil

■ Split the grouse and wash them completely. Season by rubbing them with salt and white pepper. Heat about an inch of vegetable oil in a large sauté pan, then sear the grouse halves on both sides before placing them in a roasting pan. Add the onion, carrot, and celery to the sauté pan and return to heat. Brown the vegetables lightly, then deglaze the pan with cider.

■ Scrape the bottom of the pan to get all flavors and ingredients that may have stuck. Pour the contents into the roasting pan with the grouse and cover tightly. Cook in 300° oven for approximately 1-1/2 hours, then remove from the oven. Take the birds out of the roasting pan and set them aside, keeping them warm. Place the juice and vegetables in a food processor and puree, then strain through a strainer. Return the liquid to the roasting pan and continue to heat on the stove at a medium setting until it reaches a thicker consistency, then whisk in whole butter.

To serve: Pour sauce on a plate and place the grouse over the sauce. Drizzle the grouse with additional sauce. Delicious when served with wild rice or teaberry rice.

For Simplicity's Sake:

Whether it's called ruffed grouse or partridge, few would disagree over the superb taste of the meat. A simple preparation for a special meat that needs nothing more. The grouse can be ordered pre-cleaned and split.

Stuffed Guinea Fowl
with Cream Sauce

Submitted by Peter Pagonis • Zorba's Restaurant • Brookfield, Wisconsin   *Serves Four*

Guinea Fowl

4 breasts 5 to 6 ounces each, cleaned
    and trimmed
3 bunches fresh spinach, chopped
8 scallions, chopped fine
1 tsp fresh dill, chopped fine
⅛ tsp pepper
⅛ tsp thyme
½ tsp fresh garlic, minced
1 tbsp chicken base (bouillon cube)
2 tbsp olive oil

Egg Wash

4 eggs
feta cheese, crumbled

■ Sauté the scallions and spinach until limp and tender, then add dill and seasonings. Set aside and let cool. Blend egg wash ingredients until firm. Stuff guinea fowl with the spinach mixture, roll in the egg wash, and lightly flour. Lightly brown the guinea fowl in a hot sauté pan with oil. Finish in a 375° oven until cooked through (160° internal temperature). Add sauce (below) and heat in oven for five more minutes.

Cream Sauce

1½ cups milk
¼ pound butter
½ cup butter
fresh garlic to taste, minced
white pepper to taste
¼ pound feta cheese, crumbled
1 tsp white wine

■ Make a roux (thickening agent) with equal parts of the butter and flour. Sauté until golden blond with a nutty aroma. Bring the milk to a simmer in a double boiler, add wine and seasonings, then add roux to lightly thicken. When finished, add feta cheese.

To serve: Remove pan from oven. Slice guinea fowl and place on plate, covering the meat with cream sauce.

For Simplicity's Sake:

The Greek cheese, "feta," brings flavor and an interesting texture to the egg wash, which in turn lends definition and character to the dish. While you're making roux (see glossary for definition), stir often so the flour and butter mix is not scorched. To prepare chicken stock or bouillon, see "Basic Recipes."

Napolean of Sautéed Chukar Partridge with Sweet Potato Tortillas

Submitted by Larry Brown • Black Bass Hotel • Lumberville, Pennsylvania   *Serves Four*

Chukar Partridge

4 breasts with wing joint and skin,
    cleaned and trimmed
4 sage leaves
¼ cup white wine
¼ cup extra virgin olive oil
salt and black pepper
clarified butter

■ Place one sage leaf between the breast meat and skin. Pour the wine and olive oil over the breasts, and marinate for six hours.

■ To cook partridge, remove from the marinade, pat dry, sprinkle with salt and cracked black pepper. Heat a sauté pan and coat the bottom of it with the clarified butter. When the pan is hot, put the breasts skin-side down in pan, shake the pan gently to ensure that the skin will not stick, and sauté for one minute. Turn breasts over, put them in the pan, and finish in a 400° oven until medium rare and tender (internal temperature 120° to 130°). Remove from the oven, let cool, then remove skin.

Sweet Potato Tortillas

1 sweet potato
1 egg yolk
¼ cup all-purpose flour
¼ cup chestnut flour
½ tsp salt
¼ tsp white pepper

■ Bake the sweet potato in a 400° oven for 30 minutes, then let rest for five minutes. Scoop out the meat of the potato and push it through a strainer to remove any lumps. Add the yolk and flours when the pulp is cooled to room temperature. Season with salt and white pepper. On a greased sheet pan, spread the potato batter into six six-inch wide circles of 1/8" thickness. Bake in a 375° oven for eight minutes. When done, peel the potatoes off the sheet pan and refrigerate until cool and firm.

■ Heat oil in a frying pan to fry the sweet potatoes, turning often, browning them on both sides. This should take about 45 seconds. Remove and place them on a paper towel. Sprinkle with salt and pepper.

Jus

1 ounce dried morels
1 ounce sun-dried cranberries
1½ cups water
1 cup port wine
1 cup chicken stock
6 sage leaves
salt and black pepper to taste

■ Soak the morels overnight to rehydrate. Then strain out the mushrooms and reserve the water. Add port wine to the water, place on stove, and reduce by one-half. Add the chicken stock and simmer for six to eight minutes. Then add the morels and cranberries to the sauce. Remove from heat.

Napolean Layers

2 bunches arugula, cleaned and
    trimmed
2 tbsp clarified butter
½ cup foie gras, Grade A
chestnut flour
½ cup wild rice, washed
1½ cups water
¼ cup chicken stock
bouquet garni
salt and pepper to taste

▇ Put the wild rice in a pot of water. Season with salt and pepper and bring to boil. Reduce heat and simmer for approximately 40 to 45 minutes, or until done.

▇ Cut foie gras in half, season with salt and cracked black pepper, and dust with chestnut flour. Place foie gras in a hot sauté pan with butter, and sauté until each side is lightly brown. Place on paper towels.

To serve: Spoon the wild rice on plate. Top with a pinch of arugula. Place sweet potato tortilla on top of arugula and partridge breast on tortilla. Top with a second pinch of arugula, and top this with a slice of foie gras. Spoon the sauce around on the plate.

For Simplicity's Sake:

The bird goes by different names, yet the meat is consistently delicious. There are many steps to this recipe, but it's great fun to prepare. The result is a good-tasting, distinctive meal. Cultural diversity is embodied by the sweet potato tortilla. Chestnut flour can be ordered from specialty stores, but you can also use mushroom dust or wild rice flour. Dried morels are far easier to locate than the fresh item. Instead of dried cranberries, you can use fresh or frozen berries. See "Basic Recipes" for the chicken stock. Foie gras adds a nice texture and flavor, but if you don't have it on hand, try the recipe without it.

Partridge with Cornbread-Truffle Stuffing
Served with Poached Pear and Tomato-Onion Tower

Submitted by Alisdair MacLean • The Fredonia Hotel • Nacogdoches, Texas　　　　　*Serves Four*

Partridge

4 whole, semi-boneless partridge, cleaned and trimmed
2 cup demi-glace or brown sauce
2 tbsp pommery mustard
salt and pepper to taste

■ Clean and remove each wing of the partridge. Stuff each partridge with 1/2 cup of stuffing (see right). Place in pot and put in 300° oven for 45 minutes. In the same pot, place two cups of demi-glace and return pot to oven for 15 minutes. Then remove birds. Strain stock into a sauce pan and add mustard. Bring to boil and reduce by one-half.

Cornbread and Truffle Stuffing

½ red bell pepper, diced
½ green bell pepper, diced
¼ onion, diced
¾ cup chicken stock
1 tbsp fresh sage, chopped
1¼ cup day-old cornbread, ground
1 tbsp truffles, chopped
salt and pepper to taste
2 eggs, whole

■ Beat eggs in with stock, then add all ingredients, mixing well. Check seasoning, cover, and refrigerate for one-half hour.

Poached Pears

2 peeled pears, halved and deseeded
2 cups red wine
1 tbsp sugar

■ Add sugar to a pot and place on burner. Allow the sugar to caramelize (brown). Add the wine and pears, and cook for approximately 45 minutes until pear is tender. Remove pear from liquid and slice to fan out. Set aside.

Tomato and Onion Tower

2 roma (plum) tomatoes, sliced ⅛" thick
1 onion, sliced ⅛" thick
1 sprig fresh thyme, chopped
1 tbsp olive oil
1 tbsp fresh garlic, chopped

■ Place sliced onion and tomatoes on sheet tray. Season each slice with salt, pepper, thyme, and garlic. Then stack five high, starting with the onion and alternating onion and tomato slices. Brush with olive oil and bake in a 250° oven for 30 minutes. Remove from oven and set aside

For Simplicity's Sake:

This recipe marries the flavors of mustard, cornbread, and poached pears to achieve great flavor and texture. Tomato onion is a colorful, stylish addition. You can replace pommery mustard with a grain mustard like country dijon. Allowing the sugar to caramelize will give the poaching liquid a dark, rich character. To fan the pear, make a number of perpendicular cuts, moving from side to side. Start slicing about half an inch from the top of the pear. When you press on the pear, it will fan out naturally.

To serve: Pour the sauce on a plate. Fan the pear out on the plate, then place the tomato and onion tower on the plate in an organized fashion. Slice the partridge to expose the dressing, and place the meat atop the sauce. Drizzle the sauce over the partridge.

Pan-Roasted Stuffed Pheasant Breast with Marjoram,
served with Spicey Beet Confit, and Smokey Pheasant Broth

Submitted by Patrick D. Dobbs • Caves Valley Golf Club • Owings Mills, Maryland   *Serves Four*

Stuffed Pheasant Breasts

2 whole baby pheasants (breasts removed, carcasses reserved for the broth, and leg and thigh meat reserved for the stuffing–see left)
1 sprig marjoram, chopped
⅓ cup parsley, chopped
1 egg
2 tbsp lemon zest
½ cup whipping cream
pinch nutmeg
1 tbsp ruby port wine
salt and black pepper to taste
¼ cup carrot, finely diced
¼ cup celery, finely diced
1 tsp butter

▰ Grind the leg meat in a meat grinder. Place in a food processor and blend with the egg, seasonings, zest, and herbs. Remove and place in a chilled bowl over ice. Slowly whisk in the whipping cream until light and fluffy. Sauté the vegetables in butter and cool. Then add to the previous mixture. Season.

▰ Pound the pheasant breast lightly with a meat hammer, and divide the mixture among the breasts. Roll and tie them. Sear in a heavy skillet, then finish roasting in a 375° oven until firm—about eight minutes. Remove from the oven and allow to rest.

Smokey Pheasant Broth

carcasses of the pheasants
6 shallots, finely chopped
1 carrot, finely chopped
½ celery stalk, finely chopped
1 smoked ham hock, small
2 sprigs thyme
3 juniper berries, crushed
1 bay leaf
½ cup ruby port wine
1 cup chicken stock

▰ To make the broth, chop the carcasses and sear them in hot oil in a heavy sauce pan until lightly browned. Add the ham hock, vegetables, and spices and sweat gently for approximately three minutes. Pour off the fat and deglaze the pan with the wine. Bring to boil and simmer for 15 minutes, then add the stock with an equal amount of water and simmer another 20 minutes. Strain through a fine strainer and reduce further to desired flavor. Adjust seasonings.

Spicey Beet Confit

2 tbsp butter
1½ cup red beets, julienned
2 garlic cloves, peeled and minced
2 tsp Szechwan peppercorn, ground
1 tsp sugar
½ cup red wine vinegar
1 tbsp parsley, chopped
salt to taste

▰ Add butter to a sauté pan. When sizzling, add the beets and cook 2 to 3 minutes. Season with garlic, Szechwan pepper, salt, and sugar. Toss gently and add the red wine vinegar. Simmer until the liquid is almost gone. Adjust seasonings and add the parsley.

To serve: Slice the stuffed baby pheasant breast and fan out on the plate. Add confit to the plate, and drizzle the pheasant with broth.

For Simplicity's Sake:

This is a good use of the whole bird, and the spicy beef confit provides a natural, sharp contrast. To prepare a chicken stock, see "Basic Recipes." To peel a garlic clove, place the clove on a counter and press down on the clove with the flat side of a knife. The skin will crack and come loose easily.

Pheasant a la Normande

Submitted by Claude Courtoisier • Hunter's Hollow Inn and Restaurant • Labadie, Missouri

Serves Two

1 apple, peeled and quartered
¼ cup heavy cream
2 tbsp calvados brandy
15 green peppercorns
1 2½-pound pheasant, cleaned &
   trimmed
salt and white pepper to taste
3 tbsp vegetable oil
3 tbsp butter

To prepare the apples, sauté them with one tbsp of butter for ten minutes at 450°. Remove from the oven and set aside.

Prepare the pheasant by heating two tbsp of oil and the remaining butter in a skillet. Season the pheasant with salt and pepper and place it skin-side down in skillet. Roast in oven for ten minutes at 475°. After the pheasant has roasted, remove it from skillet and discard grease. Combine brandy and cream and reduce to a thick and creamy consistency by cooking on stovetop at medium heat.

To serve: While the sauce is reducing, slice the dark meat of the pheasant. Fan the slices on a plate. Repeat the procedure for the white meat of the pheasant, placing it atop the dark meat. Sprinkle green peppercorns over the pheasant. Arrange apple quarters on the plate at the sides of the pheasant, to represent wings. Spoon the sauce over the pheasant and serve with rice pilaf.

For Simplicity's Sake:

Many people feel that pheasant is the most desirable of all game birds. This recipe offers a simple, delicious means of preparing it. Green peppercorns are purchased fresh in a can.

Wild Pheasant Breast Saltumbuca
served with Ratatouille and Creamy Soft Polenta

Submitted by Aaron Aversa • Public Landing Restaurant • Lockport, Illinois *Serves Four*

Pheasant

6 pheasant breasts
24 fresh and large sage leaves
12 slices prosciutto ham, thin
8 tbsp butter
1 cup dry white wine
¼ cup lemon juice, fresh-squeezed
4 tbsp capers without juice
½ cup all-purpose flour

■ Cut the pheasant breasts into six pieces each and use a meat hammer to pound the pieces into medallions. Place 1/2 slice of prosciutto and 1 medium-sized sage leaf on each pheasant medallion. Dust this side of each medallion with flour. Preheat skillet and melt one tbsp of butter in skillet. Place pheasant medallions, prosciutto and sage side down, in skillet. Brown lightly on this side only. Remove from skillet and set aside.

■ To make sauce, return skillet to burner, adding two ounces of white wine. Reduce by half, add one tbsp of butter, and reduce by half again. Add lemon juice and reduce for ten seconds, then add capers. Set aside for serving.

Ratatouille

1 cup Spanish onion, diced
1 cup zucchini, diced
1 cup yellow squash, diced
1 cup eggplant, diced and soaked in water
1 cup plum tomato, peeled and diced
1 cup red bell pepper, diced
1 cup green bell pepper, diced
2 tbsp fresh oregano
1 tbsp fresh basil
6 leaves fresh parsley
4 ounces olive oil
2 cups tomato puree
8 garlic cloves, chopped
1 tbsp salt
1 tsp pepper

■ Brown garlic in a sauce pan. Add eggplant, onion, squash, green and red bell peppers, and sauté for two minutes. Add tomato puree and sauté until vegetables are tender.

Creamy Soft Polenta

1½ cups yellow cornmeal
4 cups heavy cream
8 ounces cream cheese, chunked
¼ cup parmesan cheese, shredded
1 tbsp salt
1 tsp pepper

■ Bring cream to a boil in a sauce pan. Whisk in cream cheese, parmesan, salt, and pepper. Then whisk in the cornmeal until creamy.

To serve: Spoon polenta on center of plate. Fan pheasant slices in overlapping fashion around polenta. Spoon sauce over pheasant, and serve ratatouille on side.

For Simplicity's Sake:

Here's a traditional recipe adapted for the popular, sweet-tasting pheasant. The prosciutto ham, capers served with ratatouille, and creamy polenta make this recipe a sophisticated triumph. If you go the distance, you'll create a splendid, memorable meal. While you're making the polenta, continue whisking the cornmeal to ensure that it comes out creamy smooth and lump-free.

Caramelized Maple-Glazed Quail

with Pear and Parsnip Bavarian, and Smoked Tomato and Wild Rice Onion Salad

Prepared by Andre D. Halston, C.C.C., C.E.C. • Ritz Carlton Hotel • Philadelphia, Pennsylvania
1995 FINALIST – (DID NOT COMPETE)   *Serves Four*

4 pieces boneless quail
½ cup maple syrup
2 pieces ripe passion fruit
8 sage leaves
12 chives
12 sprigs thyme
8 sprigs dill
2 Idaho potatoes
3 tsp cayenne pepper
1 medium sweet red onion
6 small roma tomatoes
4 green onions
4 tbsp balsamic vinegar
¼ cup rice vinegar
1 pint olive oil
½ pound wild rice
6 ripe bartlett pears
1 pound fresh parsnips
12 leaves gelatin
2¾ cups heavy whipping cream
3 tbsp dijon mustard
⅛ pound spinach
⅛ pound watercress
2 pints blackberries
¼ cup honey
2 pounds yellow kernel corn, cooked
sea salt and cracked black pepper to
    taste

Corn Sauce

■ Place kernel corn, two tsp cayenne pepper, and two cups cream in a blender. Blend until smooth and push through a fine chinois. Salt to taste.

Blackberry Coulis

■ Over medium heat in a sauce pan, cook blackberries, two cups of water, and honey until reduced by three-quarters. Remove from heat. Using a blender, puree until smooth and push through a fine chinois or fine strainer. Add four tbsp of rice vinegar, or adjust the amount of rice vinegar according to the ripeness of the blackberries. If the sauce is too thick, thin it with vinegar.

Spinach and Watercress Oil

■ Blanch the spinach and watercress leaves by partially cooking them in boiling water, then shocking with cold water. When cooled, strain and squeeze out all water. Place in a blender, add eight tbsp of olive oil, and puree. (This could take up to five minutes.) Add sea salt and pepper to taste.

Smoked Tomato and Wild Rice Onion Salad

■ Wash the tomatoes and cook the wild rice until al dente (firm in center). Place in a smoker at 200° for eight minutes of heavy smoke (or smoke on grill). Remove the rice and allow the tomatoes to smoke five to eight minutes longer, then remove from smoker. Peel, deseed, and julienne four of the tomatoes. Fine dice the other two tomatoes, and add them to four tbsp of olive oil. Add one sprig of chopped thyme, plus sea salt and pepper to taste. Peel the red onion to get four very small, 1/4" thick rings the size of a quarter. Grill and toss in two tsp balsamic vinegar. Cut the green onions salpicon eight pieces, 1-1/2" long. Put these in ice water and allow them to curl (about eight minutes). Combine the julienned tomatoes with smoked wild rice, green onions, and red onion rings. Add salt and pepper to taste.

Pear and Parsnip Bavarian

■ Peel and remove core of pears. Dice and poach the pears in water until soft. Peel and dice the parsnips. Cook in salted water until soft, then drain. Puree the pears and parsnips in a blender (one-half liter of puree is required). Soak the gelatin leaves in cold water until very soft. Remove water and dissolve the gelatin in a microwave, then add to puree. Stir until blended. Whip 3/4 quart of cream to soft peaks. Season the puree to taste with salt, pepper, and dijon mustard. Fold in the whipped cream. Spread evenly onto a parchment paper-lined sheet pan and let cool. Cut into desired shapes.

Potato Wafers

■ Peel potatoes and slice them lengthwise into paper thin chips, two per plate. Fry until golden brown. Immediately upon removing from oil, sprinkle with cayenne pepper and sea salt. Place on paper towel.

Quail

■ Wash and dry the quail, then split into two pieces down the center and along the back. Allow the quail to sit in maple syrup for 30 to 60 minutes. Heat a sauté pan until smoking. Add four tbsp olive oil and sear the quail on both sides quickly, caramelizing the coating. Place on a rack on a sheet tray, and cook in 400° oven for five minutes.

Garnish

■ Make the garnish with two sage leaves, two chives, two sprigs dill, and two sprigs thyme per plate. Tie each with a blanched chive at the bottom, cutting the excess close to the knot. Serve one per plate. Split the passion fruit in half and spoon out the seeds and pulp of the fruit.

■ To create the finished entree, flood the bottom of a 12-inch plate with corn sauce. Place a tsp of the diced, smoked tomato at four spots around the plate, close to the border. Place one tsp of the seasoned spinach and watercress oil at two opposing spots (for example, three o'clock and nine o'clock) close to the edge of the plate, avoiding the smoked tomato. Using a teaspoon, drizzle the blackberry sauce at three or four spots on the plate. Place a shaped piece of the Bavarian at the center of the plate. Atop the Bavarian, place julienned smoked tomato, red onion ring, green onions, and smoked wild rice salad to about 1-1/2" in height. Place two of the seasoned potato chips on the salad, centering each chip. Center two pieces of caramelized quail on top of the chip. Spoon one tsp of the passion fruit pulp over the quail, and place the herb garnish next to the quail. Serve immediately. Best when accompanied by a flavorful chardonnay.

Honey Tangerine Quail with Sweet Potatoes Anna

Submitted by Nicholas Petti • Cafe Trio • Chapel Hill, North Carolina   *Serves Four*

Quail

8 semi-boneless quail, cleaned
salt and pepper to taste
■ Season the quail with salt and pepper, brush it with the glaze (below) and grill to medium rare.

Honey/Tangerine Glaze

½ tsp butter
3 tbsp shallots, minced
1 cup tangerine juice
⅓ cup honey
1 cup chicken stock
■ Sweat the shallots in butter until translucent. Add tangerine juice and reduce by half. Add honey and chicken stock, reduce by three-quarters or until glaze is thick.

Sweet Potatoes Anna

1 sweet potato, peeled and sliced ⅛"
thick
3 tbsp butter
¼ cup parmesan cheese, grated
salt and pepper to taste
■ Melt butter in a sauté pan. In a pie pan, arrange the slices of sweet potato in a layer. Pour one-third of the butter and sprinkle one-third of the parmesan cheese over the potatoes. Repeat the process two more times, then bake in a 350° oven for 10 to 15 minutes or until the potatoes are tender.

To serve: Arrange the quail on top of the sweet potatoes, and garnish with tangerine segments and fresh vegetables.

For Simplicity's Sake:

A sweet and mild approach that enhances the delicate, nutty flavor of quail. See our "Basic Recipes" section to prepare the chicken stock. This recipe will work with mandarin oranges if tangerines are not in season, and an assortment of juices can be used.

Pan-Braised Quail with Mango Jus
served with Wild Rice-Orzo Pilaf

Submitted by Robert Carter • Cafe Marquesa • Key West, Florida   *Serves Four*

Quail

8 semi-boneless quail
½ pound boudin sausage (can
substitute chorizo sausage
    or any cooked sausage)
salt and white pepper to taste
4 tbsp vegetable oil

■ Stuff each quail with sausage. Secure the legs with toothpicks, and season each quail with salt and white pepper. Set aside.

Mango Jus

2 tbsp mango vinegar (or white wine
    vinegar)
1 cup fresh mango, peeled and diced
¾ cup chicken stock
¾ cup demi-glace or brown sauce

■ Puree half the mango in a food processor and set aside. Heat a sauté pan, add vegetable oil, and heat until smoking. Brown both sides of the quail in hot oil. Deglaze the pan with vinegar and turn the quail breast-side down in the pan. Add mango puree, demi-glace, and chicken stock, and stir well. Transfer the pan to a 425° oven and cook until done, approximately 10 minutes.

Wild Rice-Orzo Pilaf

1 tbsp olive oil
½ tsp garlic, minced
¼ cup red onion, finely diced
1 cup mushrooms, sliced
¼ cup chicken stock
½ cup sweet pepper mix (red, yellow,
    green), diced
¼ cup blanched carrots, diced
1 tsp fresh thyme, chopped
1 tsp fresh chives, chopped
1 cup wild rice, cooked
2 cups orzo, cooked
salt and white pepper to taste

■ Heat a sauté pan with oil. Add the red onion and garlic, and sauté for one minute. Add mushrooms and sauté for one more minute, then deglaze the pan with chicken stock. Add peppers, carrots, thyme, chives, orzo, and wild rice. Sauté for five minutes, then adjust seasoning with salt and pepper.

To serve: Place a bed of pilaf on the plate and set the quail on top. Add diced mango to the jus and ladle on the plate. Serve with your favorite green vegetable.

For Simplicity's Sake:

You can pick up boudin sausage at your favorite butcher, or you can stuff with your favorite sausage. Mango jus lends a lighter touch to this dish, but you can substitute plums or even papaya. When buying wild rice, avoid the black grains. Look for light brown to brown long grains. In some cases, wild rice is graded. Grade A is the best, but there is no real oversight of the grading process. See "Basic Recipes" for preparation of the wild rice, and also for demi-glace or brown sauce.

Roast Quail Stuffed with Rabbit and Rice Mousseline
served with Dried Cherry and Mignotte Pepper Vinaigrette

Submitted by Mark W. Herndon • Williamsburg Inn • Williamsburg, Virginia   *Serves Four*

Quail

4 quail, cleaned and trimmed

4 slices bacon

salt and white pepper to taste

■ Stuff the quail with mousseline (right) until filled and firm. Adjust so the wing tips are tucked under and the legs are crossed on top. Use one slice of bacon per quail to wrap the entire length of the body, and secure it with a toothpick. Season the quail on all sides with salt and white pepper.

■ Place the quail on a sheet pan and roast for approximately 20 minutes in a 375° oven. Cook until firm (internal temperature of 140°), then remove from oven. Take out toothpick and discard bacon. Serve while quail is hot.

Rabbit and Rice Mousseline

1 6-ounce boneless chicken breast, cubed

1 whole egg

4 ounces heavy cream

1 tsp salt

⅛ tsp white pepper

1 tbsp fresh herbs (basil, sage, and thyme), chopped

6 ounces rabbit meat, cleaned and small-diced

½ cup wild rice, cooked

⅓ cup white rice, cooked

¼ cup blanched spinach, drained and chopped

¼ cup shiitake mushrooms, sautéed and diced

1 tbsp sun-dried tomatoes, julienned

2 tbsp pine nuts, toasted

1 whole egg

salt and white pepper to taste

■ Grind the chicken and place in a food processor. Process chicken with egg until smooth. Add heavy cream, salt, white pepper, and fresh herbs, and process until blended. Remove from processor and fold in the remaining ingredients.

Dried Cherry and Mignotte Pepper Vinaigrette

⅛ cup raspberry vinegar

⅛ cup sherry wine vinegar

½ tbsp shallots, minced

¼ tbsp garlic, minced

¼ tbsp ground peppercorns

2 tbsp dried cherries

½ tbsp fresh herbs (basil, sage, and thyme), chopped

¾ cup olive oil

salt to taste

sugar to taste

■ Lightly sauté the shallots and garlic in olive oil. Place the shallots and garlic in a bowl. Add raspberry and sherry wine vinegars, ground peppercorns, cherries, and fresh herbs. Slowly whip in the olive oil to form a temporary emulsion. Season with salt and sugar to taste.

Salad Mix

8 cups mesclun greens, rinsed and
drained

1 small radish sprout

2 6-inch corn tortilla, julienned and
fried

8 radishes

12 chives, chopped

4 sprigs basil (optional)

▨ Mix all ingredients well.

Matchstick Vegetables

16 haricots vertes, trimmed and
blanched

16 carrots, julienned and blanched

16 rutabagas, julienned and blanched

To serve: Toss the greens in vinaigrette until lightly coated, then arrange greens on top half of plate. Toss the matchstick vegetables in a small amount of vinaigrette and arrange them on bottom half of plate. Garnish the salad mix with radish sprouts and radishes, corn tortillas, chives, and basil. Slice the quail in half, placing it on top of the vegetables and next to the chilled salad. Drizzle additional vinaigrette around the plate and over the quail.

For Simplicity's Sake:

This isn't the first time we see the sweet, nutty flavor of quail coupled with the mild tastiness of rabbit. Mousseline is an elegant name for a filling. This mousseline is filled with a variety of natural flavors, and the pinenuts are a smooth complement. You can add your own twists to the salad mix and vegetables, but I heartily recommend vinaigrette with the squab. For the vinaigrette, you can replace half the olive oil with a slightly thickened vegetable or chicken stock. To roast pinenuts, simply place them on a sheet tray in a 350° oven and roast until they're golden brown. You may use greens of your choice.

Quail Filled with Pilsner Rabbit Sausage and Shiitake Schmaltz Sauce

Provided by Christopher P. Ray • Flat Creek Eatery and Saloon • Hayward, Wisconsin   *Serves Four*

Quail

4 semi-boneless quail, cleaned and
   trimmed

■ Fill the quail with two ounces of the sausage filling (see below). Clip one joint from wing and tuck the wings under the body. Slice a small hole in one leg, sticking the other leg through the hole to create a criss-cross pattern. Lightly oil and roast in a 375° oven for 12 to 15 minutes. Remove from the oven and let stand for three minutes.

Pilsner Rabbit Sausage

½ pound rabbit sausage, ground
2 tbsp carrot, finely diced
2 tbsp celery, finely diced
2 tbsp onion, finely diced
2 tbsp red bell pepper, finely diced
1 tbsp leek, finely diced
¼ tsp garlic, minced
½ cup pilsner beer (Schell's or other)
dash black pepper
1 egg white

■ Brown the rabbit sausage in a sauté pan and strain. Do not wipe the pan. Add carrot, celery, onion, and red bell pepper to the same pan and sauté for two minutes. Add leek, garlic, and pilsner beer, then season with black pepper. Let simmer until all the moisture has evaporated. Remove the mixture from the pan and chill.

■ In a food processor, puree the rabbit sausage and egg white to form a paste. Remove the sausage mixture and mix it with the chilled vegetable mixture.

Shiitake Schmaltz Sauce

1 tbsp butter, melted
4 tbsp onion, julienned
1 cup August Schell Schmaltz Alt
   beer (or any dark malt beer)
6 sun-dried tomatoes, julienned
½ cup shiitake mushrooms,
   destemmed and julienned
½ cup brown sauce
2 tbsp whole butter
1 tbsp parsley, chopped

■ Soak the sun-dried tomatoes in brandy for one hour. Heat melted butter in a sauté pan, add onions, and caramelize. Add 1/4 cup of beer and reduce until nearly dry. Strain the sun-dried tomatoes, add them to the sauté pan with the shiitake mushrooms, and sauté for one minute. Add the remaining beer and reduce by one-quarter. Add the brown sauce, then roll the whole butter in flour and stir it into the pan. Let thicken to a medium consistency, then season with salt and pepper. Add chopped parsley and stir just before serving.

For Simplicity's Sake:

An interesting combination of two beers in two aspects of this recipe, plus two game meats. The four flavors, along with the shiitake mushrooms, create a perfect marriage of simple flavors on the plate. For the brown sauce, see "Basic Recipes."

To serve: Slice the quail at an angle down the middle, to expose the filling and colors. Place on plate and top with 1/4 cup of sauce.

Applewood Roasted Squab with Foie Gras and Black Walnut Crepe

Submitted by David Daggett • Game Sales International • Loveland, Colorado   *Serves Four*

Squab

¼ squab, boned and split in half
2 tbsp dijon mustard
⅛ cup olive oil
pinch of kosher salt
pinch of black pepper

■ Rub the squab inside and out with the dijon mustard, then coat it with olive oil and season. Roast the squab over applewood embers in a barbecue grill.

Crepe Batter

¼ cup black walnuts, chopped fine
¼ cup tart apples, minced
1 tbsp chives, chopped
1 tsp honey
pinch of kosher salt
pinch of black pepper
½ cup flour
2 eggs
⅔ cup milk
1 tbsp melted butter

■ In a mixing bowl, combine walnuts, apples, chives, honey, salt, and pepper. Mix in the flour, then the eggs. Slowly whisk in the milk, then the butter. Pour the crepes into an oiled or greased sauté pan, as if making very thin pancakes about four inches in diameter. When browned on both sides, remove from pan, cover, and keep at room temperature.

Foie Gras

8 ounces foie gras, sliced ¼" thick
pinch of kosher salt
pinch of black pepper
1 shallot, minced

■ Sear the foie gras on both sides in a very hot sauté pan (approximately 30 seconds per side). In a food processor or blender, combine foie gras, salt, pepper, and shallot. Process the mixture until smooth. Place a spoon of the foie gras mixture in the center of each crepe. Fold the crepe in half, then in half again.

Sun-Dried Tomato Relish

½ cup sun-dried tomatoes, soft, julienned
¼ cup red onion, ¼" julienned
1 tsp chives, chopped
¼ cup olive oil

■ Combine all ingredients and mix them well.

To serve: Reheat the crepes in a 400° oven until warm through. Set on plate, place the squab so it overlaps the crepe, and garnish with the sun-dried tomato relish.

For Simplicity's Sake:

A nice, light dijon crust that tastes great made on the grill or broiled in the oven. The crepe is wonderful, and can be made without the foie gras spread. You can also use fresh plum tomatoes to make the relish.

Pan-Seared Squab Breasts

served over Wilted Baby Spinach with Warm Brandied Apple Mint Dressing

Submitted by Darryl R. Start • Innisbrook Hilton Resort • Tarpon Springs, Florida   *Serves Four*

Marinade

2 tbsp canola oil

4 tbsp garlic, minced

½ cup onion, minced

½ cup applejack brandy

1 cup apple juice

½ cup mint vinegar

½ cup fresh mint, minced

2 tbsp black pepper, cracked

▪ Hat oil in a sauce pan. Sauté garlic and onion, then add brandy and reduce by three-quarters. Add apple juice and mint vinegar, and reduce for five minutes. Add mint and cracked pepper. Remove and cool.

Squab

8 squab breasts, skin-on

▪ Remove excess skin not directly covering the breast meat. Place in marinade for 12 to 48 hours. When ready to cook, sear the squab skin-side down in a hot sauté pan for two to four minutes, until golden brown. Turn meat over and place it in a roasting pan. Finish in a 350° oven for three to five minutes.

Warm Brandied Apple Mint Dressing

¾ cup red delicious apples, diced

½ cup Granny Smith apples, diced

⅓ cup garlic, minced

⅓ cup fresh mint, chopped

¼ cup brandy

¼ cup sugar

1 cup apple cider vinegar

¾ cup walnut oil

▪ Heat two tbsp of oil in a sauce pan and sauté garlic. Add apples and sauté one to two minutes. Add sugar and deglaze the pan with brandy. Let simmer for two to three minutes. Remove from heat, then add vinegar and mint. Whisk remaining walnut oil in slowly.

Salad

1 pound baby spinach

4 ounces watercress

4 ounces radicchio

2 ounces frisee lettuce

▪ Remove stems from spinach and watercress. Shred radicchio and frisee. Wash, dry, and toss in 3/4 cup of warm dressing.

To serve: Place wilted greens on plate. Slice the squab and place it over the greens. Pour warm dressing down the center of the squab.

For Simplicity's Sake:

Squab dates back to the 18th century, and many would argue that this delicacy was the first bird to be served "under glass," predating the pheasant. Squab is at its finest when served rare. If you can't find mint vinegar and you don't want to make your own, substitute apple cider vinegar. You'll find walnut oil in supermarkets and specialty stores. Because this group of greens is particularly bitter, it does a nice job of cleansing the palate. However, you can assemble any combination of greens you prefer.

Roast Garlic and Fig-Braised Squab

Submitted by Danny Mellman • The Green House at Thistle Lodge • Sanibel, Florida   *Serves Four*

Squab

4 squab, boned
½ cup butter, clarified
½ tsp salt and pepper
½ cup flour
1 bunch Swiss chard
½ pound apple smoked bacon, diced
1 pint pearl onions, peeled
5 cups chicken stock
½ cup dried figs, split
½ cup Merlot
2 bulbs garlic, roasted
1 cup basmiti rice, cooked

Foie Gras

½ pound foie gras (Grade A)
2 tbsp black pepper, cracked

■ Salt, pepper, and flour the squab. Brown the squab in a heavy pot, then remove from pot. Add bacon and lightly brown. Toss in the pearl onions, figs, and garlic, and sweat for two minutes.

■ Place the squab back in the pot with Swiss chard to cover, then add the stock and wine. Cover and cook in a 400° oven for approximately ten minutes, or until squab is tender.

■ To prepare the foie gras, heat a large frying pan just before serving. Slice the foie gras into eight equal pieces, sprinkle with cracked black pepper, and sear on each side very quickly—perhaps 30 seconds per side.

To serve: Place a scoop of cooked basmati rice on the plate. Mound the swiss chard on the rice. Split the squab down the center and set atop the greens. Spoon the fig and onion from the sauce around the plate. Place two pieces of the foie gras overlapping on the side of the plate. Drizzle the remaining liquid from the pot over the squab.

For Simplicity's Sake:

It has been said that the most effective way to cook squab is roasting it. Here, roasting the delicacy in its pan-made sauce utilizes all flavors. Braising with moist heat helps the Swiss chard. Foie gras could be considered optional, but it's delightful with this sauce.

Basic Recipes

In this section, we offer directions for preparing common, "foundational" sauces and foodstuffs that are featured in a number of the book's recipes.

Cornstarch slurry

To prepare this thickening agent, use equal parts of cornstarch and water. Mix them together to create a paste. Add this slurry to a boiling liquid sauce and let simmer. You'll want to allow the pasty taste to cook out.

Puff pastry

Your basic puff pastry includes one cup of butter, two cups of sifted cake flour, and 1/2 cup of ice water. Allow two-thirds of the butter to become softened, and hand-blend the remaining butter with the flour, using two knives or a pastry cutter. Add only enough ice water to hold the ingredients together. Roll the dough out to a thickness of 1/4 inch, spread two-thirds of the dough with softened butter, and fold the remaining one-third over the buttered two-thirds. Spread butter on the top part of the pastry, then fold again. You now have three layers and all three layers are buttered. With the buttered side down, wrap in waxpaper and chill thoroughly by refrigerating for up to 24 hours. Cut into individual pastries and roll each one out. The pastries are ready for use.

Stocks, Glacé and Demi-glace

Make the following stocks ahead of time. If you wish, you can cook them in a crock pot while you run errands. Portion the stocks in plastic cups or ice cube trays and freeze. Now you'll have small, workable portions on hand at all times. For glacé, reduce the stock by cooking until it's smooth and syrupy. To make demi-glace, reduce stock to a tenth of its volume.

Chicken stock. You'll need three 1/2-pound chicken bones, three quarts of cold water, eight ounces of mirepoix (vegetables), and aromatic seasonings (parsley, thyme, sage, and others). Combine the bones and water in a pot, bring to a simmer, and skim off any fats that rise to the top. Keeping the stock at a simmer, add the mirepoix and the aromatics. Simmer until the liquid is reduced by half, then strain the stock and set aside the liquid. A suggested mirepoix: 50 percent onions, 25 percent carrots, and 25 percent celery (chopped). You can also use leeks.

Vegetable stock. Use two tsp olive oil, one tbsp chopped garlic, two tbsp chopped shallots, seven quarts cold water, one cup dry white wine (optional), 3/4 cup chopped carrot, 1-1/4 cups chopped mushrooms, 3/4 cup chopped celery, 1/3 cup chopped fennel (if available), one tbsp juniper berries, three peppercorns, three bay leaves, and aromatic seasonings.

Heat the olive oil in a pot, then add garlic and shallots. Sauté until shallots are translucent, add the rest of the ingredients, and bring to a boil. Reduce the heat to a simmer and cook for one hour. Strain and set the liquid aside.

White stock. The ingredients: two pounds of bones, six cups of cold water, 1/2 cup of mirepoix, and aromatic seasonings. Combine the bones and the water in a pot. Bring it to a simmer and skim off any fat that rises to the top. Add the mirepoix and the aromatics one hour before the stock is done. For beef bones, simmer seven to nine hours; for veal bones, six to eight hours; for chicken bones, two to four hour. For a darker, richer-tasting version of this cloudy stock, you can brown the bones and add red wine to deglaze the pan.

Game stock. You'll need two cups mirepoix, one tbsp olive oil, 2-1/2 pounds scrap meat (wings, legs, backs, necks, and trimmings), one bay leaf, one whole clove or 1/2 cinnamon stick, two black peppercorns, two quarts cold water, and aromatic seasonings. Heat the olive oil in a pot and add the meat scraps. Begin to brown them, then add the vegetables. Caramelize (brown) the vegetables, and add cold water with the aromatics, peppercorns, clove, and bay leaf. Bring to boil, then reduce heat and simmer. Reduce the stock for two to three hours, skimming off any fat that rises to the top. You may use any meat to make game stock—venison, wild boar, buffalo, pheasant, and others.

Brown sauce (or stock). Suggested ingredients: two ounces olive oil, 2-1/2 cups mirepoix (including leeks), 1/2 cup tomato sauce, ten ounces red wine, one tbsp minced shallots, one tsp minced garlic, one bay leaf, one tsp dried thyme, four quarts beef stock, and 1/4 cup cornstarch slurry (see above).

Heat the olive oil in a pot. Add the mirepoix and caramelize (brown). Add the tomato sauce cook until caramelized or until it turns bronze. Add 1/3 cup of the wine and reduce until dry. Add the same portion of the remaining wine two more times, reducing until dry. Add the stock and

spices, bring to simmer, and reduce the liquid by one-quarter. Add the cornstarch slurry and let thicken, simmering for ten minutes. Strain and set the liquid aside.

Sauces (or Bouillon) from the Store. You can buy bases, stocks, broths, and bouillon cubes in a number of flavors, including chicken, beef, shrimp, clam, turkey, vegetable, and more. Consult your butcher or order them direct. We suggest finding a base that doesn't contain MSG.

Wild rice

To prepare wild rice, let it soak overnight in cold water. Then rinse it well, place it in a casserole dish and add just enough fresh water to cover the rice. Cover the dish and bake at 350 degrees until the liquid is gone. The overnight soaking doubles your yield, and permits the rice to cook more evenly.

If you cook the rice on the stovetop without soaking it, rinse one cup of wild rice. Place it in a pan with 3-1/2 cups of cold water. Add a dash of salt, bring the water to a boil, stir well, and reduce the heat to a simmer. Cover and cook for approximately 45 minutes, or until the kernels puff

open. For a chewier texture, cook the rice for a shorter time.

If you cook in the oven without soaking, use the same portions of rice and water. Cover and place in a 350-degree oven for one hour. Add more water if needed, then stir and cook for one more hour. The wild rice should be moist, not dry.

If you're cooking in a microwave oven, use the same portions of water and wild rice. Place in a covered, microwaveable casserole dish and cook at high setting for five minutes, then cook at medium temperature for 30 minutes. Let stand for 10 to 15 minutes, then drain.

Smoking

You can smoke a food product by using one of the many home smokers on the market. You can also buy wood chips of assorted "flavors" and add them to your smoldering barbecue coals. This adds a smoked flavor to your grilled meats.

Roasting nuts

Place nuts on a sheet tray and roast in a 375-degree oven until they are golden brown. You may have to turn the nuts.

Glossary of Ingredients and Cooking Terms

Adobado. A sour paste used to marinate skirt steak or similar cuts, made with vinegar, chiles, and herbs.

Al dente. French term describing the consistency of food cooked to a tender firmness, or "just right."

Anaheim chile. A long red pepper, formerly called "Texas Long Green." Can be picked red or green.

Ancho chile. Dried, fat chili pepper with a reddish black color and a smokey taste.

Andouille sausage. A highly seasoned, hard-smoked Cajun sausage.

Anise. A spice related to parsley and native to several Mediterranean countries, with a pronounced licorice flavor.

Arrowroot. A starch similar to cornstarch, used as a thickener. However, arrowroot is flavorless. Never bring a food product to a boil once you've added the arrowroot.

Arroz. Spanish term for rice.

Au jus. In natural juices.

Bard. To wrap meat or poultry in thin layers of fat before cooking, in order to ensure moistness.

Barley. A bland-flavored grain with an extraordinary capacity for absorbing flavors mixed with it. Barley's protein quality is higher than wheat.

Baste. To brush or spoon drippings or a prepared mixture intermittently over meat, while the meat roasts.

Blanch. To partially cook food in boiling water, then chill the food with cold or icy water in order to stop the cooking process.

Blend. To mix the ingredients thoroughly.

Boudin. A pork- and rice-based sausage, highly seasoned, common in southern Louisiana.

Bouquet garni (or sachet). A bundle of herbs in a tightly tied cheesecloth sack, used to flavor stews and sauces. A coffee filter can be used instead of cheesecloth.

Braise. A technique in which food is first browned, then covered with a small amount of liquid. The food is then cooked until done.

Broil. To cook with direct high heat.

Cannellini Bean. A white kidney bean popular in Italy, Greece, and France.

Caramelize. To heat dry sugar or foods containing sugar until brown and a caramel flavor has been achieved.

Caul Fat. The outer intestinal lining of a pig, sheep, or cow, often wrapped around meats or other ingredients. The fat melts as it is cooked.

Cepes. A type of dried mushroom.

Champignons. French word for mushrooms.

Chanterelles. A group of mushrooms having a thick, meaty texture, excellent flavor, and, in some varieties, an odor of apricots.

Chiffonade. To roll leaves as if making a cigar, then slice the leaves very thinly with a knife.

Chipotle. Dried and smoked jalapeno pepper.

Chiles. Popular capsicums. These peppers range from mild (poblano) to hot (jalapeno and serrano) to the hottest known chile (habanero).

Chorizo. A spicy, dried sausage made with pork, sweet red peppers, garlic, and hot peppers.

Cilantro. A leafy green herb also known as coriander or Chinese parsley.

Clarify. To remove the solids from meat stock or melted butter, thereby making it clear. To clarify butter, heat it until foam or solids appear (this is the whey). Then skim the foam from the top.

Compote. A mixture of fresh or stewed fruit.

Concasse (or concasser). To skin, deseed, and roughly chop a tomato.

Confit (Confiture). To cook food thoroughly to obtain the consistency of marmalade; or the marmalade-like substance itself.

Cornstarch slurry. A thickening agent (see Basic Recipes).

Coulis. A puree made from vegetables, fruit, poultry, or seafood. It can stand alone or be used to flavor other dishes.

Court bouillon. A flavored liquid used for poaching that may contain wines, vegetables and spices, or herbs.

Couscous. A substance made from 100 durum wheat semolina. Couscous consists of tiny pieces of pasta.

Crepe. A thin, light pancake.

Dash. A food measurement equal to a scant 1/8 teaspoon.

Deglaze. To moisten with liquid in order to dissolve food particles or caramelized drippings left in a pan after roasting or sautéing.

Demi-glace. Literally means "half glaze." A stock reduced in volume to one-half, then to one-tenth through simmering.

Drawn butter. The American term for clarified butter, or butter from which all fat and impurities have been removed (see clarify).

Dredge. To lightly cover food with a form of breading—in other words, flour, cornmeal or bread crumbs.

Dried mushrooms. Dehydrated mushrooms. Boletus is a common, inexpensive variety that that can be used as a substitute for most others. One ounce of reconstituted dried mushrooms equals four ounces of fresh mushrooms.

Elephant garlic. A very large garlic bulb in which the cloves are shaped like elephant ears. It has a sweet and mild flavor in its raw form.

Feta cheese. A soft, crumbly, white Greek cheese made from ewe, goat, or cow's milk and pickled in brine.

Fillo. A thin, paper-like pastry originating in Greece. Most commonly used in strudel in baklava.

Foie gras. Paté made from fat liver, usually goose liver.

Fold. To combine two ingredients by turning one over the other with a spoon, using a gentle cutting and smoothing motion.

Forcemeat. A mixture of ground meat that is highly seasoned. If made with cream or egg white, it may also be referred to as a "mousse" or "mousseline."

Glacé. A stock concentrated to a syrupy consistency.

Glaze. To brush an item with butter, oil, or sauce in order to create a shine.

Five-spice powder. A Chinese spice blend containing equal parts of powdered anise, cinnamon, fennel, ginger, and clove.

Gorgonzola. An Italian blue cheese, named after a town near Milan.

Gratine. To brown quickly.

Gruyere cheese. A name given to both Swiss and French cheeses made in the Gruyeres Valley, which is shared by both countries. The cheeses have a creamy texture.

Haricots vertes. New World kidney, navy, pinto, or black beans. The term also refers to very thin, fresh beans.

Hoisin sauce. Chinese soybean and pepper sauce.

Jicama. A juicy, nutritious root native to Mexico and the American southwest. It is often called the "Mexican potato."

Julienne. To slice into very thin, matchstick-like pieces.

Juniper berries. Berries that grow on several varieties of evergreen trees. Juniper is the dominant flavor in gin, and the berries are often used in game dishes. The berry looks like a peppercorn.

Jus. Natural juices.

Mace. A spice with a strong nutmeg flavor.

Masa. A coarsely ground corn flour.

Mince. To cut into extremely small pieces.

Mirepoix. A mixture of chopped vegetables such as onions, celery, carrots and leeks, used to make soup stock.

Mole. A dark, rich brown sauce of Mayan origin.

Monter. To aerate by whisking.

Morel. A rare and expensive variety of mushroom, nicknamed "sponge mushroom."

Orzo. A small pasta shaped like barley.

Pancetta. An Italian bacon. Most commonly used is the pancetta arrotolata—bacon rolled and cured, but not smoked. There are five varieties.

Paysanne. Peasant-style vegetables cut into small squares.

Pince. To caramelize an item by sautéing. The term usually refers to tomato products.

Pinenuts. Known as pignoli or pinyons, these are blanched pine cone seeds. They give food a rustic, aromatic flavor.

Poblano. Small, mild, dark green pepper of pleasant taste.

Porcini. The "king of mushrooms"—a European mushroom revered for its meaty flavor.

Port. Portuguese wine, named because it was originally shipped from the city of Oporto.

Prosciutto. An Italian ham, salted and air-cured. The three styles of prosciutto ham are prosciutto crudo, fresco, and cotto.

Puff pastry. A pastry that "puffs" or rises (see Basic Recipes).

Puree. To process food until it assumes the consistency of a fine paste. This can be done with a food mill, a food processor, or a blender.

Quinoa. A vitamin-rich grain (pronounced "keen-wah"). The antiplano variety is slightly sweet and succulent with a pale ivory color.

Ragout. A simmering of food to create a thick, seasoned stew.

Radicchio. A small, red chicory with red and white leaves. Radicchio is crisp and bitter.

Reduce. To rapidly boil or simmer a liquid until the volume is decreased, the liquid thickens, and its flavor is concentrated.

Rehydrate. See "steep."

Render. To free fat from connective tissue by heating until the fat melts. The drippings are drained off.

Rind. The outer covering of fruits, particularly citrus fruits and melons.

Risotto. An Italian style of cooking arborio rice. The technique releases a generous amount of starch, creating a well-bound and sticky texture.

Roulade. To roll in the fashion of a jelly roll, slicing to reveal the colors.

Roux. A thickening agent consisting of equal parts of flour and butter. It is browned and cooked.

Sachet. See "Bouquet garni."

Sear. A technique using high heat to seal in the juices of a cut of meat or seafood by browning the food rapidly. Searing can be done in a skillet or in the oven.

Semolina. The gritty, grainy part of wheat, frequently used to make pastas.

Serrano. A fiery hot, flavorful green chile pepper.

Sevise. Italian term referring to a squab or small pigeon.

Shiitake. The literal translation is "oak fungus." Shiitake mushrooms are considered essential by Chinese and Japanese chefs.

Simmer. To keep a liquid at a temperature just below its boiling point, so that bubbles form only at the edges of the pan.

Steam. To cook food using the vapor of a liquid, usually water.

Steep (or rehydrate). To soak a food in liquid in order to soften or tenderize it, or so it absorbs the flavors of the liquid.

Stocks. Basic liquids or broths (see Basic Recipes)

Sweat. To cook without color. To sweat vegetables, sauté them in a pan until the moisture begins to seep out.

Truffles. Varieties of underground fungi that must be "smelled out" by trained dogs, pigs, or goats. Truffles are one of the world's gourmet delights.

Waterbath. To place a pan containing food in a pan of boiling water, then place both pans in the oven. The procedure cooks food evenly via moist heat.

Wasabi powder. Wasabi is a Japanese horseradish root. Wasabi powder is often used in Japanese cuisine.

Zest. Grated citrus rind without the white pith. Zest contains aromatic oils that give flavor to foods.

Wild Game and Specialty Foods Purveyors

Here is a listing of game and specialty foods purveyors—wholesalers, retailers, and service organizations. Contact any of these organizations directly for further information.

Aidells Sausage Company
618 Coventry Road
Kensington, CA 94707
(415) 863-7485
Smoked game sausages

The Game Exchange
107 Quint St.
San Francisco, CA 94124
(415) 282-7878, 800-GAME-USA
Large supplier of wild game, specialty items.

Venison America
Route 2, Box 2660
Elk Mound, WI 54739
(715) 874-6856

Farm Raised Foods
P.O. Box 696
Forest Lake, MN 55025-0696
(612) 464-6424

Rocky Mountains Natural Meats
6911 N. Washington
Denver, CO 80229
800-327-270
Venison

Galley Meats
610 S. Arroyo
Pasadena, CA 91101
Buffalo meats, buffalo sausage

Stockton Poultry
(209) 466-9503
Squab, wild boar, quail, partridge and more

Buckmaster Fallow Deer
Capoli Ranch
Lansing, IA 52151
(319) 586-2590

Czimer Foods, Inc.
13136 W. 159th St.
Lockport, IL 60441
(708) 301-7152
Wide variety wild game, bear and lion

John Dewar
753 Beacon St.
Newton, MA 02159
(617) 442-4292
Wide variety game, buffalo

Wilderness Gourmet
212 S. 4th Ave., Suite 223
Ann Arbor, MI 48104
(313) 663-6987
Wide variety game products

Dole & Bailey Foodservice
P.O. Box 2405
Woburn, MA 01888
(617) 935-1234
Wide variety game products

A.M. Briggs
2130 Queens Chapell Rd. NE
Washington, DC 20018
(202) 832-2600
Wide variety game products

Maison Glass
52 East 58th St.
New York, NY 10022
(212) 755-3316
800-822-5564
Wide range of game product—mallard, goose, partridge

D'artagnan, Inc.
399-419 St. Paul Ave.
Jersey City, NJ 07306
(201) 792-0748/241-4432
800-DARTAGN

American Ostrich Association
3840 Hulen St. Suite 210
Fort Worth, TX 76107
(817) 731-8597

Breezy Hill Meat Company
P.O. Box 507
Bowie, TX 76230
(817) 872-5635
Ostrich

Macfarlane Pheasant Farm, Inc.
2821 S. US Hwy 51
Janesville, WI 53546
(608) 757-7881, 800-345-8348
Pheasant

Umayat Corp.
#400, 505-8 Ave. SW
Calgary, Alberta,
CANADA T2P 1G2
(403) 232-6662
Musk Ox

Jackson Hole Buffalo
800-543-6328
American bison, all forms

Regal Pack International
26349 Road 5
Elizabeth, CO 80107
(303) 648-3089
Ostrich

National Bison Association
4701 Marion Street, Suite 301
Denver, CO 80216
(303) 292-2833
Producer

Sonoma Foie Gras
P.O. Box 2007
Sonoma, CA 95476
707-938-1229, 800-427-4559 in CA
Foie gras and muscovy duck products

Buzzard's Roost Ranch
1778 Facendini Lane
Sebastopol, CA
(707) 823-2799
(707) 542-7570
Rabbits, ducks, geese

Grimaude Farms
11665 N. Clements Rd
Linden, CA 95236
(209) 887-3121
Muscovy ducks, ostrich, foie gras

Phuel Farms
P.O. Box 154
Sierra Madre, CA 91024
(818) 255-6856
Game Birds, buffalo, boar

S & B Farms
125 Lynch Road
Petaluma, CA 94952
(707) 763-4793
Ducks, geese, guinea hens, turkeys,
rabbits

Santa Rosa Game Birds
1077 Butler Ave.
Santa Rosa, CA
(707) 546-1776
All game birds, emu

Plantation Quail
1940 Hwy 15 S.
Greensboro, SC 30642
(800) 843-3204
Fresh quail

Culver Duck Company
P.O. Box 910
Middlebury, IN 46540
(219) 825-9537
Pekin and moulard ducks

Oakwood Game Farms
Princeton, MN
800-328-6649, (612) 223-2829
Game birds, smoked pheasant,
partridge

RC Western Meats
P.O. Box 4185
Rapid City, SD 57709
(605) 342-0322
Buffalo

Maple Leaf Farms
P.O. Box 308
Milford, IN 46542-0308
(219) 658-4121
Ducks

Foggy Ridge Gamebird Farm
Q13 Highland Rd
Warren, ME 04864
(207) 273-2357
Pheasant, chukar partridge,
bobwhite quail

L & L Pheasantry
Box 298
Heggins, PA 17938
(717) 682-9074
Game birds, rabbit

Summerfield Farm
SR 4, Box 195A
Brightwood, VA 22715
(703) 948-3100/547-9600
Game birds, wholesale and retail

Valley Game & Gourmet
615 West 100 South
Salt Lake City, UT 84104
800-521-2156
Wide variety of products and specialty
foods

Unique Foods
520 Executive Drive
Willow Brook, IL 60521
800-789-6474
Wide variety of game and specialty
foods

Wild Game, Inc.
2315 W. Huron
Chicago, IL 60612
(312) 278-1661
Wide variety of game

Broken Arrow Ranch
P.O. Box 530
Ingram, TX 78025
800-962-4263
Wide variety of game, specializing in
free-range

Game Sales International
P.O. Box 5314
444 Washington
Loveland, CO 80538
800-729-2090
Wide variety of game

Boyer Creek Ranch
Barronett, WI 54813
(715) 469-3394
Red deer venison—sausage, meat cuts,
jerky

Classic Country Rabbit
P.O. Box 1412
Hillsboro, OR 97123
800-821-7426

Manchester Farms
P.O. Box 97
Daizell, SC 29040
800-845-0421
Quail

Chieftain Wild Rice Company
P.O. Box 290
1210 Basswood Ave.
Spooner, WI 54801
800-262-6368
Minnesota-grown wild rice, specialty
grains, and beans.

Backroads Coffee and Tea
P.O. Box 1019
123 W 2nd
Hayward WI 54843
800-634-4951
Microroaster of specialty coffees,
roast and ship same day

Cameron's Coffee Company
P.O. Box 627
Hayward, WI 54843
(715) 634-3646
Wholesaler of specialty coffees

Abundant Life
244 Main
Hayward, WI 54843
(715) 634-3545
Natural and specialty foods, spices,
and herbs

Grayledge Farms
185 Marlborough Road
Glanstonbury, CT 06033
800-854-5605
Pheasant, wide variety of game meat

Grimaud Farms
1320A South Aurora
Stockton, CA 95205
(209) 466-3200
Duck and rabbit

Ostrich Processing, Inc.
P.O. Box 2155
Thomasville, GA 31799
800-262-4737

Quail International, Inc.
800-843-3204
U.S.D.A.-inspected quail

Mondo's and Sons
4225 Ranier Ave. S.
Seattle, WA 98118
(206) 725-5433/725-1565
Wide range—wines, guinea fowl,
buffalo, boar, etc.

1995 Sponsors of the Original National Wild Game Cooking Competition

Reinhart Institutional Foods
1500 St. James Street, PO Box 2859
LaCrosse, Wisconsin 54602
800-827-4010
Wayne Kolberg, Director of Sales

Ed Phillips & Sons
5400 Old Town Hall Road
Eau Claire, Wisconsin 54702
800-472-6674
P.J. Schaeffer, President/Owner

Cameron's Coffee Company
PO Box 627
Hayward, Wisconsin 54843
715-634-3646
Teresa Moone/Karla Pederson Stone

Valley Game & Gourmet
PO Box 2713
Salt Lake City, Utah 84110
800-521-2156
Davee Schuh, Owner

Lawson Enterprises, Inc., representing
Dupont Silverstone and Berndes Cast
Aluminum Professional Cookware
100 W. Main St, Suite 306
Lansdale, Pennsylvania 19446
215-855-2727 or 612-475-0654

River Farms Market
Rt. 2, Box 2105
Spooner, Wisconsin 54801
800-801-2767
Lou Schneider, Owner

Supreme Lobster & Seafood
220 E. North Ave.
Villa Park, Illinois 60181
708-832-6700
Tony Bianco, Sr., President/Owner

August Schell Brewing Co.
PO Box 580414
Minneapolis, Minnesota 55458
612-824-9731
Kelly Kuehl, National Sales Director

Lady Dianne Gourmet Desserts
Royal American Foods
131-1/2 W. Main St.
New Prague, Minnesota 56701
800-289-7437 or 612-758-2645
Stephen J. Countryman

Chieftain Wild Rice Company
1210 Basswood Ave., PO Box 290
Spooner, Wisconsin 54801
800-262-6368
Joan Gerland, General Manager

Lynn Marie's Candies
Hwy 27 So., PO Box 323
Hayward, Wisconsin 54843
800-873-8343

Gourmazing Foods
PO Box 8211
Northfield, Illinois

Index of Recipes